TYPOGRAPHIC
STYLE
HANDBOOK

ALSO BY MITCHELL & WIGHTMAN

Book Typography: A Designer's Manual, 2005

INTRODUCTION

Typography sits at the intersection between language and design. Just as language has its rules of spelling and grammar, typography has its own conventions, which have evolved over centuries. However, many of these rules are not absolute; the typographer, publisher and author can choose how type is set. These choices, and how to make them, are the subject of this book.

The *Typographic Style Handbook* is for anyone who wishes to develop a practical understanding of typography and typesetting, whether working in the publishing industry, or producing promotional material for a company or institution. For self-publishers it provides a starting point for thinking about the production of text. For publishing professionals, we hope it will prove a valuable reference and aid communication between the various departments.

About this book

The book is divided into three main sections: general typesetting, books, and businesses and institutions.

general typesetting – describes basic typesetting for a range of publications. This section includes chapters on typeface choices, punctuation, numbers, headings, lists and captions for illustrations

books and journals – details the typographic conventions found in books, for example, preliminary pages, notes, cross-references, bibliographies and indexes

corporate style – explains how the treatment of text can be incorporated into an organisation's branding guidelines to create a consistent look across all printed and online material.

Specialists in some fields, such as mathematics and chemistry, will find that we do not cover their subject in any detail as we do not have the space to do justice to the complexity of those subjects.

This handbook is intended to be used as a reference work. In order that each section is self-contained, some information is repeated.

We have also included additional explanations in some areas such as printing processes and image treatments. This is based on our experience of the addditonal requests for information and advice from clients when supplying materials to be designed, typeset and printed.

Typographic style

The concept of *typographic style* incorporates both editorial and visual conventions, from the use of punctuation to the design of a title-page. In essence, it is the idea that some typographic elements may be treated in more than one way. For example, speech can be indicated by single quotation marks:

> 'She's expecting,' Jane added, 'A girl.'
> 'How do you know?' Robert said.

or by double quotation marks:

> "She's expecting," Jane added, "A girl."
> "How do you know?" Robert said.

Both are correct. Which one you use is a matter of *style*. Having made a choice it should be applied consistently throughout the publication.

House style

A set of styles used by a particular organisation is known as their *house style*.

A house style document lists preferred typographic treatments as well as dealing with editorial matters, such as spelling, grammar and tone of voice in written text. It can also contain a section on work-progression to ensure the correct procedures are followed.

Companies may have a house style document as part of their branding guidelines. The house style creates a consistency throughout all the printed and online documents and advertising produced by a commercial organisation.

Some academic institutions create style guides for students submitting dissertations and doctoral theses, many of which are available online. These address basic typesetting issues, but are particularly concerned with the correct form of citation in bibliographies and footnotes.

See *Appendix J* (p. 266) for the authors' own basic house style, used at Libanus Press.

Why use a house style?

The aim of creating a house style is to achieve consistency throughout a publication or group of publications. This reduces distractions for the reader as inconsistencies may appear to be errors and deflect the reader's attention from the text.

Clarity and precision are of particular importance in technical works, such as medical or engineering publications, and creating a consistent text reduces the risk of confusing the reader.

In publications that include texts from a number of contributors, asking authors to follow a house style will make the production process more efficient.

Responsibility for house style

Ideally the creation of a house style should be undertaken by someone with editorial or typographic experience. Consulting publications in the same field may help the process. Many house styles evolve over time through a process of trial and error; some are the work of meticulous individuals.

However a house style has developed, it is essential to specify where the responsibility for the content of a publication lies, who has authority to make changes, and who signs off the final proofs. No one should make unauthorised changes to text.

Applying house style to a text will take time, so project managers should consider how this can be done efficiently. In most cases, getting the text as clean as possible before the design and typesetting process begins will be most cost-effective.

An important question to ask is: how far do we take the application of house style? Should every piece of paper to come out of an organisation have the same rules applied? Common sense has to prevail – there is no need to lavish the same care on an in-house e-mail as you would on the production of a book.

A trickier proposition is what to do with a text that is internally consistent, makes sense to the reader, but uses a different style to your own. Is it worth making extensive changes for the sake of house style? There is no definitive answer to this: it will depend on the priorities and resources of each organisation.

Using this book

There are three kinds of information in this book: rules, styles and principles.

Rules – these are typographic conventions that are universally used and understood in the presentation of written text. For example:

Rule   If a sentence starts with a number, the number is always spelled out:

to France. Twenty-seven of the men travelled back to Spain in the

Using figures in this situation would be wrong:

to France. 27 of the men travelled back to Spain in the summer of

We have limited the inclusion of rules to those that may be unfamiliar to the general reader. Rules that are so well known as to be obvious, such as using a capital M for Mr, have not been listed.

Styles – these are typographic conventions that vary from organisation to organisation. Accordingly we have given alternative styles.

Here we have the choice between using capitals or small capitals for the abbreviations 'BC' and 'AD' within text:

Style 1   Capitals are used:

in the sixth century BC. The Roman Empire absorbed Egypt in 30 BC, but defeated attempts at invasion in the third century AD.

Style 2   Small capitals are used:

in the sixth century BC. The Roman Empire absorbed Egypt in 30 BC, but defeated attempts at invasion in the third century AD.

In this case there are only two styles. Other text treatments will have more styles to choose from.

Principles – with some typesetting decisions, such as choosing a typeface or the amount of space between lines, there are too many possibilities to list, so we have set out the basic principles to be considered.

Choosing styles

Editors and typesetters who work on the setting of a text have to balance the reader's understanding of the text's content with the need to produce readable and visually pleasing pages. A simple example is the choice between whether or not to use full points with initials:

Style 1   Initials with full points:

> the T. S. Eliot quotations were identified by E. F. Peters in

Style 2   Initials with no full points:

> the T S Eliot quotations were identified by E F Peters in

Which is better?

On the one hand, the convention of using full points in this context is well understood by readers; it contains no ambiguities. On the other hand, Style 2 looks cleaner without the full points; the page is less spotty. How this is resolved will depend on the nature of the publication.

Content can also affect the choice of a style. Whereas short headings may benefit from the extra weight of being set in the capitals of Style 3:

Style 1   Chapter 3

Style 2   *Chapter 3*

Style 3   CHAPTER 3

a text containing long headings may be better served by the compact italic of Style 2:

Style 1   Which Moped with Chrome-plated Handlebars
                     at the Back of the Yard?

Style 2   *Which Moped with Chrome-plated Handlebars*
                     at the Back of the Yard?

Style 3   WHICH MOPED WITH CHROME-PLATED
                HANDLEBARS AT THE BACK OF THE YARD?

Practical considerations

As well as aesthetic and editorial concerns, there are practical factors to be considered when creating a house style and thinking more widely about an organisation's publications.

In publishing houses there will be editors, proofreaders, designers and typesetters all applying themselves to the task, but in other organisations it will often fall to non-specialists to oversee the production of printed and digital documents. Consider these factors:

software – what typesetting programs are available to the organisation? Word-processing programs allow much less flexibility within a text setting than specialist programs such as Adobe InDesign® and Quark XPress®. Using industry-standard software for design and layout should reduce the risk of technical confusions where the work in one program will not transfer to another.

typefaces – what fonts are available to the organisation? Not all typefaces contain the same range of characters and styles.

implementation – will the work be carried out in-house or by freelancers? Many organisations hire designers and typesetters for projects that may be beyond the skills of in-house staff.

enforcement – who will proofread publications and ensure that the house style is followed correctly? At what stage in the production process should house style be applied?

efficiency – applying house style takes time. Whilst some changes can be made globally to a text document, other changes may need to be made individually which could add to the production time and the cost.

print or screen – is the publication to be printed or published online? Consult with a printer or website-builder to ensure that you are conforming to the industry standards for creating files. Responsive websites and e-books are less fixed than printed text. How does this affect the application of a house style?

Production and work progressing

A house style document can also contain guidance on the production of text and how work is managed, both inside and outside the organisation. For example, it may include the following:

list of suppliers – such as editors, designers and printers.

paper choices – range of papers which are used by the organisation.

production schedules – for publications produced regularly.

project management – details on who is responsible for overseeing and signing off a project, and who is responsible for the day-to-day management.

instructions for archiving – how finished files are stored for the long term.

Although this is not a manual on print management, we have tried to describe some of the issues that may arise in the process of producing publications. It is advisable to establish good relationships with printers and website-builders and raise any queries you have with them at an early stage. See *Appendix A, Progressing printed works*.

Getting started

If you are new to the subject of typography, the *Basic terms of the trade* in the following pages will introduce the terminology used throughout this book. For anyone who works with, or employs, designers, typesetters, editors or printers, becoming familiar with the industry terminology will make conversations clearer and help to avoid confusions.

The chapter on *Body text* has an introductory section explaining the basic principles of typesetting.

A list of standard symbols for marking up text can be found in *Appendix C*. A list of abbreviations can be found in *Appendix F*.

A combined Glossary and Index can be found at the end of the book.

PAGE LAYOUT

In printed works a **page** refers to one side of a leaf of paper. Two pages opposite each other are called a **double-page spread**; the left-hand page is the **verso** and the right-hand page the **recto**.

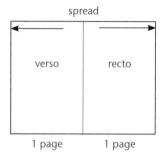

The area of the page containing the text is the **text panel**. The white areas around the edge of the text are the **margins**. The top of the page is called the **head** and the bottom is called the **foot**. The inner edge of the page is the **gutter** and the outer is the **fore-edge**.

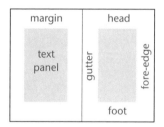

A page that is taller than it is wide is called **portrait format**.
A page that is wider than it is tall is called **landscape format**.

The same terms apply in describing illustrations.

An **upper-case** alphabet, also known as capitals or **caps:**

A B C D E F G H I J K L M N O P Q R S T U V W X Y Z

A **lower-case** alphabet:

abcdefghijklmnopqrstuvwxyz

An individual letter, mark or symbol is called a **character.** A set of letters, numbers and symbols created to a single design is called a **font.**

the font Minion Pro regular:

abcdefghijklmnopqrstuvwxyz
A B C D E F G H I J K L M N O P Q R S T U V W X Y Z
1234567890,.;:'""?!@£$%&*()[]{}\/+=

A set of fonts created around the same design is called a **typeface.**

A selection of fonts from the typeface Adobe Garamond:

ABCDEF fghijklmno123?!,
ABCDEF fghijklmno123?!,
ABCDEF fghijklmno123?!,
ABCDEF fghijklmno123?!,
ABCDEF fghijklmno123?!,
ABCDEF fghijklmno123?!,

A selection of fonts from the typeface Helvetica:

ABCDEF fghijklmno123?!,
ABCDEF fghijklmno123?!,
ABCDEF fghijklmno123?!,
ABCDEF fghijklmno123?!,
ABCDEF fghijklmno123?!,
ABCDEF fghijklmno123?!,

FONT STYLES

Many letter forms have small horizontal or slanted strokes at the end of the main strokes; these are called **serifs.** Fonts which do not have serifs are known as **sans-serif** fonts. Fonts that resemble handwriting are called **scripts.**

a font with serifs – Cycles: ABCDEabcdefghijklmnopqrstuvwxyz

a sans-serif font – Gill sans: ABCDEabcdefghijklmnopqrstuvwxyz

a script – Lucida handwriting: *ABCDEabcdefghijklmnopqrstuvwxyz*

A font in which the main strokes are straight and vertical is called **roman**. A font in which the main strokes slope forward or are curved is **italic**.

a roman font – Collis roman
ABCDEabcdefghijklmnopqrstuvwxyz

an italic font – Collis italic
ABCDEabcdefghijklmnopqrstuvwxyz

Small caps are a set of capitals that are designed to match the visual height and weight of the lower-case alphabet when set at the same type size.

upper-case, small caps and lower-case in Bembo
ABCDEFGHIJKLM ABCDEFGHIJKLM abcdefghijklm

The **weight** of a font is determined by the thickness of the strokes. The most common weights are **light, regular, semi-bold** and **bold**.

from light to bold in Stone Sans
ABCDEabcdefghijklmnopqrstuvwxyz
ABCDEabcdefghijklmnopqrstuvwxyz
ABCDEabcdefghijklmnopqrstuvwxyz
ABCDEabcdefghijklmnopqrstuvwxyz

Text fonts are designed especially for setting long texts to be read continuously, such as books. **Display fonts** are designed for use in headings, title pages and covers.

text fonts – Garamond Pro and Cycles regular
ABCDEabcdefghijklmnopqrstuvwxyz
ABCDEabcdefghijklmnopqrstuvwxyz

display fonts – Bauer Bodoni black and Rialto italic
ABCDEabcdefghijklmnopqrstuvwxyz
ABCDE*abcdefghijklmnopqrstuvwxyz*

Lining figures are numbers that are uniform in height.

0123456789

Non-lining figures or **old-style figures** are numbers that vary in height and alignment.   0123456789

Both lining and non-lining figures may also be referred to as **Arabic numerals** in contrast to **roman numerals** such as II, IV, XII, iii, ix, xvi

Superior or **superscript** characters are printed smaller and higher than regular characters.

abcdefgh^ijklmnopq rstuvwxyz

Subscript characters are printed smaller and lower than regular characters.

abcdefgh_ijklmnopq rstuvwxyz

SPECIAL CHARACTERS

Marks that are added to letters to change the sound are **diacritics**.

À Á Â Ã Ä ě é É È Å Ď ď Ď Ð đ Đ ű ų ų

More commonly used ones are referred to as **accents**.

Characters outside the usual set of letters, numbers and punctuation marks are called **special sorts**. They may include mathematical or phonetic symbols and ornamental characters.

∏ ∞ ≠ ◌ § ¶ ‰ → † ◌

Where two or more characters are joined together, this is called a **ligature**.

ct fb ffb ffi ffj ffk fft fi fj sp st

SPACING

Space added between individual characters is called **letterspacing** or **kerning**. Space added between lines of type is called **leading**. The space between two words is a **word-space**.

The size of type is measured in **points** (pt). The measurement is taken from the top of the **ascenders** to the bottom of the **descenders**.

Type sits on an imaginary line called the **baseline**. The height of the lower case alphabet without ascenders or descenders is the **x-height**.

The space between lines of type is called **leading**. It is measured in points from baseline to baseline.

abcdefghijklm
nopqrstuvwxyz
abcdefghijklm
nopqrstuvwxyz
11 pt type on
11 pt leading, also
known as **set solid**

abcdefghijklm
nopqrstuvwxyz
abcdefghijklm
nopqrstuvwxyz
11 pt type on
13 pt leading

abcdefghijklm
nopqrstuvwxyz
abcdefghijklm
nopqrstuvwxyz
11 pt type on
15 pt leading

An **em** is a unit of measurement equivalent to the size of type; so in a text set in 10 pt, an **em space** is 10 pt wide and an **em dash** is 10 pt long.

An **en** is a unit of measurement equivalent to half the size of type; so in a text set in 10 pt, an **en space** is 5 pt wide and an **en dash** is 5 pt long.

em space   en rule

The width of a panel of text is the **measure**.
When text is aligned down the left-hand side it is **ranged left**.
When text is aligned down the right-hand side it is **ranged right**.
Text that is aligned down both sides is **justified**.

abcdefghijklm	abcdefghijklm	abcdefghijklm
nopqrstuvwxyz	nopqrstuvwxyz	nopqrstuvwxyz
abcdefghijklm	abcdefghijklm	abcdefghijklm
nopqrstuvwxyz	nopqrstuvwxyz	nopqrstuvwxyz
ranged left	ranged right	justified

Indenting a line of text means to start it inside the left margin of the text panel.

He had dreamt once of writing novels, but had not achieved so much as a novella, in spite of all the unfinished manuscripts lying around in folders. But unfinished they

A hung out line of text starts outside the left margin of the text panel.

He had dreamt once of writing novels, but had not achieved so much as a novella, in spite of all the unfinished manuscripts lying around in folders. But unfinished they were

Turning over a word means moving it from the end of one line to the beginning of the next line.

before   He had dreamt once of writing novels, but had not achieved so much as a novella, in spite of all the unfinished manuscripts lying around in folders. But unfinished they were fated to

after   He had dreamt once of writing novels, but had not achieved so much as a novella, in spite of all the unfinished manuscripts lying around in folders. But unfinished they were fated to

Taking back a word means moving it from the beginning of one line to the end of the previous line, the opposite of the action shown above.

In general, books are divided into three parts:

The preliminary pages, or **prelims**, contain, for example, the title page, imprint page and contents page.

The **main text** is the main body of the text.

The **endmatter** contains additional information such as appendices and index.

Possible preliminary pages:	Possible endmatter pages:
half-title	appendices
frontispiece	notes
title page	glossary
imprint page	bibliography
contents page	picture sources
acknowledgements	index
preface/foreword	colophon
list of illustrations	note on the type used

The main text may be divided into **chapters** or **parts**.

A **chapter** usually starts on a new page with a **chapter heading**.

A **part** is indicated by a recto page called a **part-title**, containing the number of the part, with the text starting on the following spread.

The main text excluding headings and footnotes is called the **body text**.

Chapter Three heading

body
text
He had dreamt once of writing novels, but had not achieved so much as a novella, in spite of all the unfinished manuscripts lying around in folders.

Where the title of the publication and the chapters are repeated at the top of each page, these are called **running heads**.

PAGINATION

Pagination is the numbering of the pages. A page number is called the **folio**.

The first page of the publication – not including the cover – is page 1. All pages are included in the **pagination**, whether or not they have printed folios.

A publication may be numbered throughout using Arabic numerals, or the preliminary pages may be numbered in roman numerals with Arabic numerals starting from 1 on the first page of the main text. Page 1 is always on a recto.

1	half-title		i	half-title
2	frontispiece		ii	frontispiece
3	title-page		iii	title-page
4	imprint page		iv	imprint page
5	contents page		v	contents page
6	blank		vi	blank
7	main text starts		1	main text starts

A page containing no text or images is called a **blank** and has no folio but is counted in the total of pages.

PRINTING AND BINDING

A black and white image that contains shades of grey is a **half-tone**.

The printing of coloured images is done using four colours – cyan, magenta, yellow, black – and is called the **four-colour process**.

Spot colours are mixed separately and printed in an additional print run; this is often used in commercial branding.

Books are printed on large sheets of paper, printing 16 pages (8 per side) or more. These are then folded into sections called **signatures**.

The card covering of a paperback publication is called the **cover**. The binding of a hardback publication is called the **case**. The paper wrapper that is sometimes placed around the binding is the **jacket**. The papers that attach the case to the pages of the book are the **endpapers**.

A **perfect-bound** publication has pages glued down the spine. In a **thread-sewn** publication, each signature is sewn together and then glued down the spine. A short publication that is stapled is called **saddle-stitched**.

General typesetting

BODY TEXT

INTRODUCTION TO SETTING BODY TEXT

This section refers to the setting of continuous prose, in paragraphs. Other forms of text are dealt with in later chapters.

Readability

The key concept when setting body text is that of readability, particularly for extensive texts that will be read for long periods. Good readability means that the eye moves along the lines of text without distractions.

Readability is determined by the relationship between a number of factors: choice of font, type size, length of line, word-spacing and leading. As with many aspects of typography, it cannot be achieved by applying set rules or formulae. It is created using the visual judgement of the designer/typesetter.

Text fonts

There are many fonts designed for setting body text, and within this range characteristics may vary significantly. Some fonts are more suitable for setting, for example, at larger sizes or in narrow columns. If choosing one *house font* for body text in all your publications, it should be tried out in a variety of sizes and layouts to ensure that it has the required versatility.

As a rule, text fonts with serifs have better readability than sans-serif fonts for long passages of continuous text because the horizontal serifs help the eye along the line. The clarity of a sans-serif font may be more suitable for some purposes and can be easier on the eye for people with reading difficulties. In this handbook, which is designed as a reference book, a sans-serif font is used to contrast with the serif fonts in the examples.

Type size

Body text should be set at a size that is comfortable to read for the appropriate length of time. For a novel, which may be read for hours at a time, using the right type size will stop the reader from getting tired. A short leaflet, on the other hand, may be set at a smaller size. The function of the text should determine the size of the type.

Body text at 10.25 pt; footnotes at 8 pt:

issued soon after the first, he added the phrase, 'by the Creator' to his final sentence, thereby readmitting the notion of the divine agency.[3]

Despite this and other alterations, Darwin's theories undermined orthodox religious teaching, chiefly because *On the Origin of Species* was

2. For futher explanation of this subject, see Chapter 8, pp. 315–18.

3. Op cit, pp. 275–6.

Body text at 8 pt:

Contacting the company
For further information about guarantees, or to enquire about a service, please telephone us on one of the numbers below.

Code of practice
Our partners have a statement describing services to customers. This can be downloaded from our website.

Complaints
If you have a complaint, please telephone us on the number below.

The visual size of a typeface is determined by the x-height and width of characters, so the point size is not a useful indicator of how large it will look.

Garamond, 20 pt   abcdefgh abcdefgh   Lexicon, 20 pt

abcdefghijklmnopqrstuvwxyz   abcdefghijklmnopqrstuvwxyz

Garamond, 10 pt   Lexicon, 10 pt

Type size and leading

The following examples are set in 10 pt type with leading at 14 pt:

Garamond, 10 pt type on 14 pt leading:

He had dreamt once of writing novels, but had not achieved so much as a novella, in spite of all the unfinished manuscripts lying around in folders. But unfinished they were fated to remain, he having been unlucky with his muses, they, for some reason, having never tarried long enough with his

Lexicon, 10 pt type on 14 pt leading:

He had dreamt once of writing novels, but had not achieved so much as a novella, in spite of all the unfinished manuscripts lying around in folders. But unfinished they were fated to remain, he having been unlucky with his muses, they, for some reason, having never tarried

Leading between lines helps keep the eye moving along the line. Too little leading and the eye can drift to the line below. Too much leading and it is harder for the eye to locate the start of the next line quickly. Both of the above settings can be improved by an adjustment to size and leading:

Garamond, 11.25 pt type on 14.5 pt leading:

He had dreamt once of writing novels, but had not achieved so much as a novella, in spite of all the unfinished manuscripts lying around in folders. But unfinished they were fated to remain, he having been unlucky with his muses, they, for some reason, having never tarried

Lexicon, 9.25 pt type on 15.5 pt leading:

He had dreamt once of writing novels, but had not achieved so much as a novella, in spite of all the unfinished manuscripts lying around in folders. But unfinished they were fated to remain, he having been unlucky with his muses, they, for some reason, having never tarried long enough with

Character width and measure

The width of an alphabet in proportion to the x-height of the characters varies between fonts:

abcdefghijklmnopqrstuvwxyz   Minion

abcdefghijklmnopqrstuvwxyz   Centaur

Narrow fonts are useful when setting text in a narrow measure or when there is a need to reduce the number of pages in a publication.

The optimum number of characters per line (including spaces and punctuation) for continuous justified text is 68–72. A shorter line may create uneven word-spacing. A longer line can be tiring to read for long periods and may need more leading to compensate.

50–55 characters per line:

He had dreamt once of writing novels, but had not
achieved so much as a novella, in spite of all the
unfinished manuscripts lying around in folders.
But unfinished they were fated to remain, he
having been unlucky with his muses, they, for some
reason, having never tarried long enough with his

68–72 characters per line:

He had dreamt once of writing novels, but had not achieved so much
as a novella, in spite of all the unfinished manuscripts lying around
in folders. But unfinished they were fated to remain, he having been
unlucky with his muses, they, for some reason, having never tarried

80–85 characters per line:

He had dreamt once of writing novels, but had not achieved so much as a novella, in
spite of all the unfinished manuscripts lying around in folders. But unfinished they
were fated to remain, he having been unlucky with his muses, they, for some reason,

Justified and ranged left text

There are two alignments of body text: ranged left and justified.

Ranged left:
He had dreamt once of writing novels, but had not achieved so much as a novella, in spite of all the unfinished manuscripts lying around in folders. But unfinished they were fated to remain, he having been unlucky with his muses, they, for some reason, having never tarried

Justified:
He had dreamt once of writing novels, but had not achieved so much as a novella, in spite of all the unfinished manuscripts lying around in folders. But unfinished they were fated to remain, he having been unlucky with his muses, they, for some reason, having never tarried

The advantage of ranged left setting is that the space between words remains consistent throughout. This is particularly noticeable when text is set in a narrow column. Many people who experience difficulty reading prefer ranged left setting.

The advantage of justified setting is that the eye gets into a regular rhythm reading lines of the same length. Extensive texts, designed to be read for long periods, such as novels, are usually set justified. A disadvantage is that the word-spacing needs more attention to make it as even as possible, especially in narrow columns.

Word-spacing

Ideally, the space between words should be as even as possible. In ranged left text this is easily achieved, but in justified text the space will vary line by line. Adjustments should be made, using the layout program's justification settings and manual adjustments if necessary, to ensure even spacing. Attention should be paid to tight and loose lines appearing close together.

1.1 Text design

1.1.1 *Individual and series designs*

Publishing houses will often design books individually to produce a text style that is sympathetic to the book's subject matter, or they may have a template design for each series.

Commercial organisations and companies may wish to use a consistent text style for their printed and on-line documents as a way of reinforcing their branding.

Style 1   Use the same body text design for all publications produced by the company or institution.

Style 2   Use a different body text design for each publication, choosing a style that is appropriate to the content of the individual publication.

Style 3   Use a different body text design for each publication, but keeping within a family of styles that are recognisably from the same publisher.

1.1.2 *Body text and display text*

A publication may be made up of many different typographic elements, such as body text, headings, captions, etc. Each element should be treated consistently throughout the publication.

As a rule, keeping the number of type styles to a minimum will give the cleanest look to a design.

Style 1   Use one typeface for body text and all other elements:

HEADING	Albertina, 16 pt caps
Sub-heading	Albertina, 12 pt italics
Body text	Albertina, 10 pt roman
captions	Albertina, 9 pt italic
notes	Albertina, 8 pt roman

Style 2   Use one typeface for body text, captions and notes, and a second
typeface for headings:

HEADING	Rialto, 20 pt caps
Sub-heading	Rialto, 16 pt italics
Body text	Albertina, 10 pt roman
captions	Albertina, 9 pt italic
notes	Albertina, 8 pt roman

Style 3   Use one typeface for body text, a second typeface for headings,
captions and notes:

HEADING	Stone Sans, 16 pt caps
Sub-heading	Stone Sans semi-bold, 10 pt roman
Body text	Albertina, 10 pt roman
captions	Stone Sans, 8 pt roman
notes	Stone Sans, 8 pt roman

The treatment of these various elements is dealt with in more detail
in later chapters.

See 7.2 *Headings and sub-headings.*

See 8.2 *Captions.*

See 14.2 *Notes in general non-fiction.*

NOTE TO 1.1.2
In Style 2 the font used for the headings, Rialto, is quite decorative, but not
appropriate for notes, so the body text font is used for all smaller text.

In Style 3 the font used for the headings, Stone Sans, is very legible at smaller sizes
so may be used for captions and notes.

1.2 Choosing a font for body text

The body text is a good starting point when designing a publication.

The following factors should be considered:

readability – how easy is the typeface to read?

typeface family – how many different fonts are available within the typeface family and how legible are they?

accents and special sorts – will the text include accents, foreign characters or mathematical symbols?

weight – how dark or light does a page of text look? Is the font too light at smaller sizes?

column width – how many words will fit in a line of text?

Rule Use the same font for body text throughout the publication unless changes are requested by the author.

1.2.1 Readability and body text

In organisations that use a particular font as part of their branding, it may be advisable to choose a roman text font for setting longer texts, keeping the brand font for headings, etc. (see 15 *Corporate style*).

Italic fonts are not usually chosen as the principal font for body text.

Sans serif fonts are often specified for informational publications and forms where universal accessibility is particulary important as they are clearer for people with visual impairments or reading difficulties (see *Appendix G*).

Style 1 Use a serif font for body text.

Style 2 Use a sans-serif font for body text.

Style 3 Use the company's brand font for body text

Style 4 Use a specially designed text font for body text

1.2.2 The typeface family

A typeface chosen for body text should have, at least, the following range of fonts:

regular (may also be known as roman, book, text or bib)
abcdefghijklmnopqrstuvwxyz ABCDEFG

italic (may also be known as oblique or sloped)
abcdefghijklmnopqrstuvwxyz ABCDEFG

semi-bold
abcdefghijklmnopqrstuvwxyz ABCDEFG

semi-bold italic
abcdefghijklmnopqrstuvwxyz ABCDEFG

small caps (may also be known as expert or caps)
ABCDEFGHIJKLMNOPQRSTUVWXYZ

small caps italic
ABCDEFGHIJKLMNOPQRSTUVWXYZ

old-style and lining figures as alternatives
0123456789   0123456789

Many italic forms are narrower and darker than the roman, which can become a factor in your choice if the text contains a large number of italicised titles.

Rule   Always use proper italic, bold and small cap fonts, rather than selecting those styles in the formatting palette. This will ensure that the fonts print correctly.

NOTE TO 1.2.2
Names may vary. Fonts called *medium* may be equivalent to *regular* or *semi-bold* in other typefaces and are sometimes a weight in between the two. Typefaces which have a large number of weights may reject the usual naming conventions entirely. For example, the typeface Lexicon has Lexicon A (the lightest) to Lexicon F (the heaviest).

Special sorts

If a text contains unusual accents, characters or symbols it may be necessary to use a specialist font. However, some text fonts contain a much wider range of characters than others, and this should be considered when choosing a font for body text.

Before setting a text, it may be useful to do a trial conversion between the word-processing document and the layout document to ensure the transition between programs and fonts occurs without the loss or incorrect replacement of characters.

Cyrillic capitals
АБВГДЕЖЗИЙКЛМНОПРСТУФХЦЧШЩЪЫЬЭЮЯ

Greek capitals
ΑΒΓΔΕΖΗΘΙΚΛΜΝΞΟΠΡΣΤΥΦΧΨΩ

fractions
⅓ ⅔ ⅛ ⅜ ⅝ ⅞ ¼ ½ ¾

special sorts
é ê ë è ē ĕ ę ě ń ņ ň ĥ ū ŭ ů ű ų ź ż ž ǿ ð Đ ħ þ

ligatures
ꜩ fb ff ffb ffh ffi ffj ffk ffl fft fh fi fj fk fl ſp ſt

Ligatures are used to avoid clashes between lower-case characters and for decorative effect.

Measure and character width

The width of a font will have a bearing on the number of characters per line. Narrower fonts will usually set more comfortably in a narrow measure.

Rule   *Expanded* or *condensed* fonts should not be selected for setting body text.

Rule   Body text should not be distorted, either vertically or horizontally to fit a design or to resolve other typesetting issues.

Weight of body text

Typefaces vary in the thickness of the strokes that form the characters. This has an impact on the overall tone of a page of text. A page that is too pale or too dark may look unattractive and will be uncomfortable to read for long periods.

Darker fonts, such as Lexicon, tend to be more legible at smaller sizes; lighter fonts, such as Garamond, look better at larger sizes.

Garamond:

He had dreamt once of writing novels, but had not achieved so much as a novella, in spite of all the unfinished manuscripts lying around in folders. But unfinished they were fated to remain,

Lexicon:

He had dreamt once of writing novels, but had not achieved so much as a novella, in spite of all the unfinished manuscripts lying around in folders. But unfinished they were fated to remain, he having been unlucky with his

Rule   Light, semi-bold or bold fonts should not be chosen for setting body text.

1.2.6   *Colour printing and body text*

Body text is conventionally printed in black for reasons of legibility and economy. Printing text in four-colour process results in type that is not completely sharp as it is made out of dots. Printing text in an additional spot colour – for example, the red in this book – is sharp. Both methods of colour printing will cost significantly more than black-only printing.

Printing a book or long publication in a colour other than black will be off-putting for many readers. See also 10.6 *Co-edition texts*.

Style 1   Set body text in black.

Style 2   Set body text in a spot colour.

Style 3   Set body text in four-colour process colour.

1.3   Type size

The type size at which body text is set is chosen using the designer's visual judgement. The following factors should be considered:

typeface – the visual size of a font depends on its x-height. A font with a small x-height will need to be set at a larger size to be readable.

readability – the text should be set at a size that is comfortable to read for an appropriate period of time. This is the most important rule in determining type size for body text.

length of line – the optimum number of characters on a line, including spaces and punctuation is between 68 and 72. Shorter lines of justified text will have uneven word-spacing, but will still be readable. Longer lines become uncomfortable to read for any period of time.

weight – type set at a larger size will look heavier; a smaller type will make for a lighter page.

words per page – changing the size of type will change the number of words in the text panel, thus, changing the number of pages (extent) of the publication. If the extent has been specified in advance, type size is one of the factors that is used to achieve the desired number of pages. However, this should not be at the expense of readability.

components of the text – if a text contains extensive footnotes, captions or extracts which are set smaller than the body text, these should be considered when choosing the type size of the body text, as the smaller texts will also need to be set at a legible type size.

category of publication – the body text in a large illustrated book will usually be larger than that in a small informational leaflet. Familiarising yourself with a wide range of publications will help you choose a type size suited to the content.

Rule   The type size of the main text should be consistent throughout. Body text in the prelims and endmatter may be set at a smaller size.

1.4   Leading

1.4.1   *Specifying leading*

The following factors should be considered when specifying leading:

length of text – leading plays an important part in making a text readable, and for long continuous texts particular care should be taken. Shorter texts, such as captions for illustrations, may be set a little closer.

measure – a wider text panel will need more leading than a narrow one to help the eye along the line.

weight – a darker font will need more leading than a light one so the page does not look too dense.

x-height – a font with a large x-height will need more leading than a font with a small x-height to create space between the lines.

alignment – justified text may need a little more leading than ranged left text if the word-spacing is looser.

Rule   The leading of body text should be consistent throughout the publication.

1.4.2   *Auto-leading*

Layout programs have an *auto-leading* feature, allowing the typesetter to specify a size for the leading throughout a document as a percentage of the type size, so that when the type size is changed the leading changes automatically.

This method of leading may be adequate in some circumstances but it gives the typesetter less control over the individual components within the design. If used, the ideal percentage will depend on the chosen typeface. It will usually be larger than the default 120%.

Leading can also be set by forcing the text to sit on a baseline grid within the document. This reduces the typesetter's control over individual components, but does ensure that pages *back up* (that is, that the lines of text on a page line up with the text on the reverse).

1.5   Alignment of body text

The conventional ways of setting continuous prose are ranged left and justified. See the Introduction to this chapter (p. 29) for the advantages of both.

Style 1   Use a ranged left setting for body text.

Style 2   Use a justified setting for body text.

1.6   Ranged left text

1.6.1   *Word-spacing in ranged left text*

The size of spaces between words in ranged left text is determined by the typesetting program's justification settings, specifically the optimum setting.

Rule   Word-spacing in ranged left text should be uniform throughout.

1.6.2   *The ragged right edge*

Ranged left text usually requires less manipulation than justified text, but care should be taken that the right-hand edge has a random look and doesn't create a distracting shape down the right edge of the text panel.

1.6.3   *Word division in ranged left setting*

The variation in line length in ranged left text should mean that it is not necessary to divide a word between lines. However, in a narrow column it may improve the overall look of the text to divide some longer words.

Style 1   Do not divide words from one line to the next.

Style 2   Only divide words of more than eight characters, excluding proper names.

1.7 Justified text

1.7.1 *Measure and characters per line*

The width of the text panel should be consistent throughout the publication. The optimum number of characters per line, including spaces and punctuation, is between 68 and 72.

1.7.2 *Word-spacing in justified text*

The width of spaces between words is determined by the typesetting program's justification settings. These allow the user to define a minimum, optimum and maximum width for word-spaces. These values can be adjusted for different fonts.

1.8 Manual adjustments to text

In some typesetting programs, manual adjustments may be made to justified setting by turning words over onto the next line, or by tightening up the spacing to take words back onto the previous line.

1.8.1 *Repeated words*

Rule   A word should not appear twice in a row at either end of a line.

paper. Although he had begun to have doubts about his
ability to express the thoughts to which he had given his

1.8.2 *Repeated hyphens*

Style 1   The number of hyphens in a row at the end of a line is limited to one.

Style 2   The number of hyphens in a row at the end of a line is limited to two.

announcing, in effect, his conversion. Spender, writing about the
two stories in his 1935 study *The Destructive Element*, found them religious in tone. He thought sufficiently highly of them that he submitted them, unsuccessfully, on Upward's behalf to the *Criterion*,

See also 1.9.1 *Hyphenation settings*.

1.9   Word division

When a line of type is particularly tight, the typesetting program will break the final word into two and divide it between lines:

two stories in his 1935 study *The Destructive Element,* found them religious in tone. He thought sufficiently highly of them that he submitted

The program's *hyphenation settings* determine how these breaks occur.

1.9.1   *Hyphenation settings*

The styles given here are examples: other specifications may be used if they are appropriate to the content and style of the publication.

	Style 1	Style 2
smallest word to be divided	[7]	[6]
minimum number of letters before hyphen	[4]	[3]
minimum number of letters after hyphen	[3]	[3]
maximum number of hyphens in a row	[1]	[2]
whether to break capitalised words	[no]	[yes]
whether to break the last line in a column	[no]	[no]

1.9.2   *Methods of word division*

Style 1   Divide words with reference to the *New Oxford Spelling Dictionary* (OUP).

Style 2   Divide words between syllables, ensuring that the first part of the word will be pronounced correctly when read:

oper-ation *not* opera-tion

Style 3   Divide words after a consonant.

NOTE TO 1.9.1

Dividing capitalised words should be avoided, but is permissible with longer names. Try to ensure that the first appearance of a name is not divided.

1.10 Paragraphs and sections

1.10.1 *Section breaks*

A section break is used to indicate a change of scene or subject.

Style 1   A section break is indicated with a single line-space.

Style 2   A section break is indicated by two or more line-spaces, keeping the space consistent throughout the text.

In Styles 1 and 2: where a section break falls on the first line or last line of a page, an asterisk, or other decorative device, is placed centred in the line.

Style 3   A section break is indicated by two or more line-spaces containing a decorative device. The space should be kept consistent throughout the text. The first line of the paragraph following the break is set without an indent:

Charles V, would have lent special prestige to the then small Amsterdam. In short, it was not only a trade centre but was also a focus of religious life over two centuries, a Canterbury of the Low Countries.

In medieval Amsterdam, secular authority was just as embedded in countless forms of ritual as the spiritual life. Initially quite open, the city was soon surrounded by ramparts and eventually

Rule   The first line of the paragraph following the section break is set without an indent.

NOTES TO 1.10

A minimum number of lines that can appear above or below a section break – usually 2 to 4 – should be specified.

Styles 1 and 3 can both be used in the same text if two levels of section break are required.

1.10.2 *New paragraphs*

Style 1   A new paragraph is indicated by starting the first sentence on a new line, indented from the left margin:

Orion now wants to take revenge on Oenopion, but on his quest he meets Artemis, who, like him, is obsessed with the hunt.

They hunt together, but Apollo interferes by sending a monstrous scorpion to pursue Orion. He can do nothing to defeat that hideous

The size of the indent is consistent throughout the publication.

Style 2   A new paragraph is indicated by starting the first sentence on a new line, following a line-space and set full out:

Orion now wants to take revenge on Oenopion, but on his quest he meets Artemis, who, like him, is obsessed with the hunt.

1 #

They hunt together, but Apollo interferes by sending a monstrous scorpion to pursue Orion. He can do nothing to defeat that hideous

Style 3   A new paragraph is indicated by starting the first sentence on a new line, following a half-line space and set full out:

Orion now wants to take revenge on Oenopion, but on his quest he meets Artemis, who, like him, is obsessed with the hunt.

½ #

They hunt together, but Apollo interferes by sending a monstrous scorpion to pursue Orion. He can do nothing to defeat that hideous

---

NOTES TO 1.10.2

Style 1 is the most commonly used for continuous texts.

Style 2 is commonly used in business letters, brochures and company reports.

Style 3 will make backing up (see p. 41) impossible in printed matter.

Styles 2 and 3 will cause confusion in complex texts with section breaks and sub-sections.

1.10.3   *Paragraph ends*

Rule   Where possible, the last line of a paragraph should contain at least two words.

1.10.4   *First and last lines of paragraphs (orphans and widows)*

The first line of a paragraph on the last line of a page is an *orphan*.
The last line of a paragraph on the first line of a page is a *widow*.

Style 1   The first line of a paragraph should not fall on the last line of a page.

Style 2   The first line of a paragraph can fall on the last line of a page.

Rule   The last line of a paragraph should not fall on the first line of a page.

1.10.5   *Minimum lines above and below sections and headings*

Rule   The last page of a chapter should contain a minimum of four lines of text.

Rule   Headings and sub-headings that do not fall at the top of a page should have at least three lines of text above:

Rule   Headings and sub-headings should have at least three lines of text below them (see 7.4 *Sub-headings*). If there are just one or two lines, the heading is turned over onto the top of the next page, leaving blank lines.

Rule   A section break should not have a single line of text above or below. It should either fall on the first/last line of the page or have at least two lines above and below.

NOTES TO 1.10.4

In books containing dialogue, it may be impossible to avoid widows completely. Judgement should be used to determine what is acceptable, with longer lines at the top of a page where possible.

In the UK, widows are avoided by adjusting the word-spacing of a paragraph to create or lose a line. In the US, widows are avoided by varying the number of lines on a page by one. When this method is used, both pages on a spread should be adjusted to contain the same number of lines. The leading should not be changed.

TYPE STYLES IN BODY TEXT

2.1 Roman and italic

The two basic type styles are the roman face and the italic face:

the quick brown fox jumps over the lazy dog   roman
the quick brown fox jumps over the lazy dog   italic

Continuous text is conventionally set in a serif typeface.

2.1.1 *Standard use of italics*

Rule   Italics are used for the titles of:

Books, newspapers, periodicals and journals

Films, plays and operas, T.V. and radio series, song collections

Paintings, sculptures and other works of art

The Times noted that the absence of *The Adoration of the Magi* lessened the impact.

Some foreign words are italicised (see 10.1 *Italicisation of foreign words*).

2.1.2 *Author's use of italics*

Style 1   Italics may be used in body text for emphasis:

Their behaviour here is making life *intolerable.*

When italics are applied for emphasis by someone other than the author of the original quote, this is noted in square brackets:

Their behaviour here is making life *intolerable* [my emphasis].

Style 2   Italics may be used in a novel for internal dialogue:

For ten years now people have been asking me, *Are those your teeth?* Each time, before they ask *Are those your teeth?* they say *Excuse me.*

NOTES TO 2.1.1
Titles of songs, poems and articles are not italicised, but set within quotation marks.

Style 3   Italics may be used at the first mention of a technical term:

This margin is referred to as the *fore-edge* in the binding trade.

2.1.3   *Opposite font*

Rule   Where a section of text is set entirely in italic, any words which would normally be in italic should be set in roman, the *opposite font*:

The Times noted that the absence of *The Adoration of the Magi* lessened the impact.

The Times *noted that the absence of* The Adoration of the Magi *lessened the impact.*

2.2   Bold and semi-bold

A typeface may contain semi-bold and bold fonts:

regular   **semi-bold**   **bold**

If a heavier weight is required for emphasis within body text, semi-bold is usually more legible, but this will depend on the design of the typeface.

2.2.1   *Use of bold and semi-bold in body text*

Style 1   Bold and semi-bold are not used in body text.

Style 2   Semi-bold is used to highlight words or numbers in informational publications such as guidebooks and manuals:

The stone circle is situated in the village of **Avebury**, Wiltshire.

Style 3   Bold is used to highlight words or numbers in informational publications:

The stone circle is situated in the village of **Avebury**, Wiltshire.

For use of bold in indexes, see 13.5 *Indexes*.

2.3 Capitals and small caps

2.3.1 *Use of capitals and small caps in body text*

Style 1 **Capitals are used for initials and acronyms in body text:**

Egypt in the sixth century BC. The Roman Empire absorbed Egypt in 30 BC, but rulers of Meroe defeated attempts at invasion, and the kingdom continued to thrive into the third century AD.

Style 2 **Small caps are used for initials and acronyms in body text:**

Egypt in the sixth century BC. The Roman Empire absorbed Egypt in 30 BC, but rulers of Meroe defeated attempts at invasion, and the kingdom continued to thrive into the third century AD.

Capitals and small caps both benefit from some letterspacing:

SEPTEMBER → SEPTEMBER   Caps with letterspacing added

SEPTEMBER → SEPTEMBER   Small caps with letterspacing added

See also *Appendix E.*

NOTE TO 2.3.1
Small capitals are designed to have the same weight as capital letters. Using the small cap conversion in the type palette produces a smaller and weaker interpretation. In these examples the type size is the same and the paletted small caps come first:

BC BC Minion   BC **BC** Bembo   BC **BC** Quadraat

This effect can stand out uncomfortably, especially in chapter openings with small caps. The first line has paletted small caps, the second has designed small caps:

THE YEAR THE WAR came closer I was six or seven and it did not

THE YEAR THE WAR came closer I was six or seven and it did not

2.4   Superscript and subscript

Superscript numbers are used to indicate footnotes or endnotes (see 14.5 *Note Indicators*):

army,[28] the colonel reported that the project was 'going to plan'.[29]

in reproductions of old texts:

fatto dalla Ill.[ma] S.[ria] di Venetia, nel lido; / per la felice uenuta del Ser.[mo] et Inuitiss.[o] Henrico III. Re / di Franza et di Polonia, l'anno 1574.

and – in conjunction with subscript – in scientific/mathematical texts:

H_2O C_2N_5OH H_2SO_4 $P(x) = a_0 + a_1x + a_2x^2 + \ldots + a_nx^n$

Rule   The size and height of superscript and subscript text is adjusted within the typesetting program to create the most visually pleasing and legible result. The percentages will vary depending on the font. For example:

	Size*	Position†
Superscript	70%	30%
Subscript	70%	30%

* percentage of type size
† percentage of type size above the baseline

PUNCTUATION

3.1 Full points (full stops)

3.1.1 *Abbreviations and contractions*

Abbrevitation: a word shortened by removing letters from the end.
Contraction: a word shortened by removing letters from the middle.

Rule A full point is used to indicate an abbreviation:

Capt. (Captain)   vol. (volume)   fig. (figure)   etc. (et cetera)

Rule A full point is not used with a contraction:

Mr (Mister)   St (Saint)   Sgt (Sergeant)   figs (figures)

3.1.2 *Initials and full points*

Style 1 Abbreviations consisting of initials take full points:

U.S.A.   B.B.C.   p.l.c.   R.S.P.B.   M.I.5   M.P.   B.C.

Style 2 Commonly used initials do not take full points:

USA   BBC   plc   RSPB   MI5   MP   BC

3.1.3 *Initials and names*

Style 1 Initials take full points, followed by a word-space:

J. M. W. Turner   J. K. Rowling   C. B. Fry   T. S. Eliot

Style 2 Initials take full points; there is no space between initials:

J.M.W. Turner   J.K. Rowling   C.B. Fry   T.S. Eliot

Style 3 Initials do not take full points, but are spaced:

J M W Turner   J K Rowling   C B Fry   T S Eliot

NOTES TO 3.1

There should be just one word-space between a full point and the following word.
If an abbreviation falls at the end of a sentence, a second full point is not used.
When setting an older text – for example, a 19th-century novel – the conventions of
the time, such as 'Mr.', are often used. This is a decision to be made by the editor.

3.2 Semi-colons and commas

3.2.1 *Punctuation of lists in continuous text*

Style 1 **Items in a list are divided by commas:**
biology, chemistry, astro-physics, sociology, literature, geography

Style 2 **Items in a list are divided by semi-colons:**

early printed books; humanities; medicine; science; architecture;
standard sets; 15th- to 20th-century literature; modern first editions

3.3 Ellipses and dashes

3.3.1 *Ellipses*

Style 1 **Ellipses are set as three spaced points with a space before and after,
regardless of whether they are at the end or the middle of a sentence:**

it had been very nice . . . the coffee . . . the chat . . . the cognac, of
course, and the trust he had in me . . . Plus the honour shown to my
sister . . . all extremely . . .

Style 2 **When an ellipsis falls in the middle of a sentence, it is set as Style 1.
When it falls between sentences, the previous sentence is finished
with a full point:**

and the trust he had in me. . . . Plus the honour shown to my sister

3.3.2 *Em dashes to indicate missing letters*

**An em dash is used to indicate a word or name that the author does
not wish to spell out in full:**

both the shire and the town. —shire was seventy miles nearer
London than the remote county where I now resided: that was

NOTE TO 3.2.1
Style 2 is appropriate when the list items are more complex.

3.3.3   *Em dashes and en dashes*

Style 1   Spaced en dashes are used, parenthetically, in pairs:

Yesterday's conversation – across the Pyrenees, across the Irish Sea – was about what they were reading at that moment. She

Style 2   Unspaced em dashes are used, parenthetically, in pairs:

Yesterday's conversation—across the Pyrenees, across the Irish Sea—was about what they were reading at that moment. She

3.3.4   *En dashes meaning 'to' or 'between'*

Rule   An en dash, not a hyphen, is used to indicate the word 'to':

1972–88   pp. 63–9   May–July 2012   London–Paris

If joining two phrases, rather than individual words, it is set spaced:

1 March 1970 – 6 May 1971

3.4   Brackets [square brackets] and parentheses (round brackets)

Rule   Square brackets are used to indicate an insertion into the text by someone other than the speaker or writer, to clarify meaning:

'They're crazy about culture [in Los Angeles]. Austen and

Rule   Parentheses are used for cross-references and birth/death dates:

in some cases titles (see p. 63). They can take the form of

LUDWIG VAN BEETHOVEN (1770–1827)

NOTE TO 3.3.3
Style 1 is more popular in the UK; Style 2 is more popular in the US.

NOTE TO 3.3.4
Kerning between en dashes and letters can be very close in some fonts. Use manual kerning or adjust the kerning tables to ensure they do not touch.

NOTE TO 3.4
The full point is placed outside the closing bracket unless a whole sentence is enclosed within the brackets.

3.5 Italicising punctuation

3.5.1 *When to use italic punctuation*

Rule Where the punctuation is part of an italicised phrase, it is italicised:

when *Will You Please be Quiet, Please?* was published in 1976 the

In the above example, the comma and question mark are part of the italicised title.

Where punctuation does not form part of the italicised phrase, it is set in roman, even when it is set next to an italic word:

three collections of stories, *What We Talk about When We Talk about Love, Cathedral* and *Elephant. Fires*, a collection of essays, poems and

3.5.2 *Italic brackets and parentheses*

Style 1 Brackets and parentheses are set in a roman font, even if the text is italicised:

addressing the problems of modern (*steel and concrete*) *construction*

Style 2 Brackets and parentheses are set in the same font as the rest of the text:

addressing the problems of modern (steel and concrete) construction

3.6 Compound words

Compound words are formed when two or more words are joined by hyphens:

sixteenth-century buildings up-to-date systems war-torn areas
fund-raiser bell-ringer know-how son-in-law stock-in-trade

Rule When a compound word is set on two lines, it should be divided at the hyphen and not by dividing one of the constituent words.

NOTE TO 3.6
For extensive lists of compound nouns and adjectives, *The Economist Style Guide* is a good resource.

SPEECH, QUOTATIONS AND EXTRACTS

4.1 Quotation marks

4.1.1 *Single and double quotation marks*

Style 1   Single quotation marks are used, with double quotation marks for quotes within quotes:

> On 11 April he wrote: 'Was AU really a "charlatan", simply out for fame at all costs?'

Style 2   Double quotation marks are used, with single quotation marks for quotes within quotes:

> On 11 April he wrote: "Was AU really a 'charlatan', simply out for fame at all costs?"

In the UK, the position of other punctuation marks – inside or outside the quote marks – depends on whether the punctuation itself is included in the quoted phrase. In the US the punctuation goes inside.

4.1.2 *Extensive quotations*

Rule   Where a quotation continues over several paragraphs, use an opening quotation mark at the beginning of the quotation and at the start of successive paragraphs; the only closing quotation mark is at the end of the final paragraph:

> He remarked that Yolande's father was "well known locally and highly respected.
>
> "Although [her brother] is known to possess Communist views, there is no evidence that these views are shared by his sister.
>
> "From enquiries made it appears that Yolande does not openly associate herself with any Political party or express any extreme Political views."

NOTES TO 4.1.1

When setting a text containing a lot of dialogue, choose a font in which the quote marks are not too heavy so they don't create a spotty text.

Word-processing programs may produce upright quotation marks – known as *tick marks* " ' – these are symbols for inches and feet and and should be replaced.

4.2   Dialogue

4.2.1   *Setting dialogue*

Style 1   Quotation marks, either single or double, as 4.1.1, are used to indicate dialogue. Each change of speaker is treated as a new paragraph and indented:

> "How is it you remember these dates so precisely?" the Doctor asked.
> "I always write them down."
> "Oh ... and why?"
> "I'm writing a chronicle of my master's accomplishments."

Style 2   Em dashes are used to indicate dialogue:

> — How is it you remember these dates so precisely? the Doctor asked.
> — I always write them down.
> — Oh ... and why?
> — I'm writing a chronicle of my master's accomplishments.

Style 3   Italics in continuous text are used to indicate dialogue:

> He tells the waiter, *I feel like Croatia.* The waiter tells Ludwig Jakob Fritz, *That's Mr Supilo, he's a big shot in the newspapers.* Madame comes up to Mr Supilo, because Mr Supilo asks, *Madame?* And Madame says, *Letitia is ready.*

NOTES TO 4.2.1

Style 2 is not often used, and only at the request of the author. In some cases the lack of punctuation to close the dialogue may cause confusion.

Style 3 is used only if it is the preference of the author.

4.2.2   *Speech attributions*

Rule   Where a line of dialogue is divided by the speech attribution, the first closing quote mark is placed after the punctuation of the dialogue:

'I don't care,' she said, 'what you think of it.'

4.2.3   *Unfinished sentences*

Style 1   Unconcluded lines of dialogue are indicated by an en dash preceded and followed by a word-space:

'It all depends what you want to do,' Clara intervened. 'For example, if you're a photographer – '

Style 2   Unconcluded lines of dialogue are indicated by an ellipsis preceded by a word space:

'It all depends what you want to do,' Clara intervened. 'For example, if you're a photographer . . . '

Style 3   Unconcluded lines of dialogue are indicated by an unspaced em dash:

'It all depends what you want to do,' Clara intervened. 'For example, if you're a photographer—'

See also 3.3 *Ellipses and dashes*.

4.3 Interviews

Style 1　Interviews are set with the name of each interviewee repeated in bold or semi-bold, followed by a colon, preceding their words:

> **Q:** You've managed to get out. What next?
> **Lema:** It's no problem to get past army posts in the night.
> **Q:** You mean you paid the feds on the army posts?
> **Ruslan:** We never pay to get past their posts. But we do buy weapons, of course.
> **Q:** When did you last buy weapons?
> **Ruslan:** About a month ago.

Style 2　As Style 1, but initials are used after the first occurrence of a name:

> **Q:** You've managed to get out. What next?
> **Lema:** It's no problem to get past army posts in the night.
> **Q:** You mean you paid the feds on the army posts?
> **Ruslan:** We never pay to get past their posts. But we do buy weapons, of course.
> **Q:** When did you last buy weapons?
> **R:** About a month ago.

Style 3　As Style 1 or 2, but with a different font (e.g. italic) used for the questions:

> **Q:** *You've managed to get out. What next?*
> **Lema:** It's no problem to get past army posts in the night.
> **Q:** *You mean you paid the feds on the army posts?*
> **Ruslan:** We never pay to get past their posts. But we do buy weapons, of course.
> **Q:** *When did you last buy weapons?*
> **R:** About a month ago.

NOTE TO 4.3
Using a different colour for one speaker, or for the names, can add a dramatic effect, but will add significantly to the print cost if colour is not being used elsewhere. Ensure that both text colours are equally legible.

4.4 Quotations and extracts from other texts

4.4.1 *Quotations set within continuous text*

Style 1 **The quoted text is set indented on both the left and right, and a line-space is inserted before and after. Quotation marks are not used:**

environment. At Newnham Grange she fell under the spell of the river, with its boats, bathers, arching trees and its play of light.

1#

From the big night-nursery window we could look right down onto the slow green river beneath us; and if a boat went by it was reflected upside down, as a patch of light moving across the ceiling.
    Here we were never out of hearing of the faint sound of the water running over the weir.

1#

The river flowed deep into her consciousness and later became a recurrent motif in her work.

Style 2 **As Style 1, but with a half-line-space before and after the quoted text:**

environment. At Newnham Grange she fell under the spell of the river, with its boats, bathers, arching trees and its play of light.

½ #

From the big night-nursery window we could look right down onto the slow green river beneath us; and if a boat went by it was reflected upside down, as a patch of light moving across the ceiling.
    Here we were never out of hearing of the faint sound of the water running over the weir.

½ #

The river flowed deep into her consciousness and later became a recurrent motif in her work.

Style 3   The quoted text is set indented and at a smaller size than the main text (this is called *setting down*). Leading is the same as the main text:

> environment. At Newnham Grange she fell under the spell of the river, with its boats, bathers, arching trees and its play of light.

1#

>> From the big night-nursery window we could look right down onto the slow green river beneath us; and if a boat went by it was reflected upside down, as a patch of light moving across the ceiling.
>>   Here we were never out of hearing of the faint sound of the water running over the weir.

1#

> The river flowed deep into her consciousness and later became a recurrent motif in her work.

> The leading of the quotation is kept the same, despite the smaller type size so that the main text will line up with the text on the reverse of the page (*backing up*).

NOTES TO 4.4.1

If the text after the quotation is a continuation of the paragraph before the quotation (as in the examples above), the first line is set full out. If it is a new paragraph, it is indented.

If the main text is set in a narrow column, extracts may be indented on the left but not on the right.

Style 2: The spaces before and after the quotation will have to be adjusted to a full line-space if an extract falls across two pages. This is so that the last line of text aligns with baseline of the text panel on the rest of the pages.

4.4.2 Interjections in quoted text

Rule   Words added to a quoted text by the author or editor are placed in square brackets:

and arranged for Jacques to have a room there for a week in July.

There was a garden [Jacques recollected] that stretched down to the river, bordered by old chestnut trees which trailed the

---

4.4.3 Omissions from quoted text

Style 1   Words or passages omitted from a quoted text by the author or editor are replaced by ellipses:

situations that they couldn't possibly have been published . . . I was too much interested in form for its own sake . . . I wanted my writing to be true to life and at the same time I wanted it to be

Style 2   Words omitted from a quoted text by the author or editor are replaced by ellipses in square brackets to make it clear that they are not part of the original text:

situations that they couldn't possibly have been published [. . .] I was too much interested in form for its own sake [. . .] I wanted my writing to be true to life and at the same time I wanted it to be

---

4.4.4 Errors in quoted text

Rule   If a quoted text contains spelling errors that are to be preserved, [*sic*] is inserted after the mis-spelled word:

logistics, the whole affair was organised by Sweds [*sic*]. With respect to the planning, the former head of the Norwegian legation and his

---

4.5   Letters and diary entries

Style 1   Letters and diary entries are set indented on left and right with a
line-space before and after. The positions of any greetings,
addresses, etc., are standardised throughout:

all night, dimly lit by two oil lamps, covered with a cloth of black
velvet and watched over by a guard.

> My dearest George,
>   Father was taken very ill last night with great suffering.
> They sent for Dr Moxon and he came in time to see him take
> his last breath. Mother said he was not the least afraid to die.
>   You will come at once,
>   Your HEL

By mid-morning the coffin had been moved to the porch of the
Chapter House, inside which had gathered aristocrats, statesmen,

Style 2   Letters and diary entries are set in italics with a line-space before and
after. Positions of greetings, addresses, etc., are standardised:

unresolved from their past marriage. Emotionally restrained, he was
flirtatious with ideas and relished strong intellectual relationships.

> *15 July*
> *Oeufs molles en gelée, cold salmon trout with mayonnaise, tomato and cucumber salad, strawberries arrosées in brandy & with cream; cheese; bottle of chilled Sancerre. Bruce C. very good value and should be a pleasure to teach.*

'Sotheby's is having fits, of course,' Elizabeth wrote to Gertrude. She
had left Wilson's employ after her engagement was announced.

NOTE TO 4.5
Handwritten letters and diaries are often written expressively, with phrases under-
lined or capitalised for emphasis. When reproducing these marks it is important to
keep in mind what is necessary to aid comprehension and what may be a distraction.

NUMBERS

5.1   Lining and non-lining figures (numbers)

There are two types of figures:

lining figures (also called *modern*): 01234567890

and *non-lining figures* (also called *old-style*): 0 1 2 3 4 5 6 7 8 9

Style 1   Non-lining figures are used in lines of lower-case or mixed upper- and lower-case text:

The volumes were prepared for William Grenville (1759–1834) from the existing Lysons volumes published in 1813.

Non-lining figs are used in lines of small caps:

50 · DANIEL LYSONS 1762–1834

Lining figure are used in lines of upper-case:

FRIDAY 8 JUNE, 2004

Style 2   Lining figures are used throughout.

Upper- and lower-case:

The volumes were prepared for William Grenville (1759–1834) from the existing Lysons volumes published in 1813.

Small caps:

50 · DANIEL LYSONS 1762–1834

Upper-case:

FRIDAY 8 JUNE, 2004

NOTE TO 5.1

Style 2 may be appropriate for publications such as annual reports where figures appear in the text and in tables. In this case, use lining figs throughout for consistency.

5.2 Decimals

5.2.1 *Multiple-digit numbers*

Style 1   Whole numbers which have four digits or more are grouped into threes, starting from the right, using commas:

3,128   52,662,740   91,549

Style 2   Whole numbers which have four digits or more are grouped into threes, starting from the right, using spaces:

3 128   52 662 740   91 549

5.2.2 *Decimal fractions*

Rule   Decimal fractions are indicated with a decimal point:

0.57   0.0001   0.2   91,549.07

5.2.3 *Money*

Rule   Pounds and pence are indicated with two decimal places:

£12.90   £8.40   not   £12.9   £8.4

NOTES TO 5.2.1

Style 1 is used in the UK; Style 2 is used in France and Germany.

Exceptions, set without commas or spaces, are: years, page numbers, reference numbers, mathematical workings and numbers denoting columns and lines of poetry.

5.3 Fractions

5.3.1 *Fractions within text*

There is variation in the availablity of fractions in different typefaces. Check the glyph table: they may be in the regular or expert font. If none are available, they are created by the typesetter within the layout program.

Style 1 Use fractions from within the font:

$1\frac{1}{2}$ $2\frac{1}{4}$ $3\frac{3}{8}$ $4\frac{2}{3}$

Style 2 Use fractions from within the font, set at a slightly smaller size if it improves the appearance of the text:

$1\frac{1}{2}$ $2\frac{1}{4}$ $3\frac{3}{8}$ $4\frac{2}{3}$

Style 3 Use fractions made from lining figures, reduced in size, with the denominator sitting on the baseline and the numerator raised up by baseline shift. Your layout program may have a command for making these automatically. The line between them – the fraction bar, or vinculum – is diagonal:

$1\frac{1}{4}$ $2\frac{1}{4}$ $3\frac{3}{8}$ $4\frac{2}{3}$

5.3.2 *Fractions within mathematical settings*

Fractions are set with a horizontal fraction bar:

$$\frac{1}{101} + \frac{1}{202} + \frac{1}{303} + \frac{1}{606}$$

NOTES ON 5.3.1

Kerning between whole numbers and fractions, and within fractions created by the typesetter, may need to be adjusted manually.

5.4   Weights and measures

5.4.1   *Units of measurement*

Style 1   Units of measurement are set closed up to the preceding number:

25mm   8oz   14lb   106cm   3km

Style 2   Units of measurement are set spaced from the preceding number:

25 mm   8 oz   14 lb   106 cm   3 km

Rule   Units of measurement – whether abbreviations or contractions – do not take a full point.

5.4.2   *Dimensions*

Dimensions are indicated with a multiplication sign, not the letter 'x', set spaced:

25 × 82 mm   174 × 126 mm   64 × 57 cm

According to convention, height is given before width. This can be stated in the preliminary pages of the publication. If further clarification is needed, abbreviations for height, width and depth may be used:

70(h) × 38(w) × 25(d) mm

5.5 Times and dates

5.5.1 Twelve-hour and twenty-four-hour clocks

Style 1   A twelve-hour clock is used with am and pm. Hours and minutes are separated by a colon:

8:40am   11:15am   3:00pm   10:20pm

Style 2   A twenty-four-hour clock is used. Hours and minutes are separated by a colon:

08:40   11:15   15:00   22:20

When setting a twenty-four-hour clock, the hours will always have two digits: 08:15, 03:00, etc. This is unnecessary with a twelve-hour clock.

5.5.2 Hours, minutes, a.m. and p.m.

Style 1   The am and pm are set closed up to the minutes:

8:40am   11:15am   3:00pm   10:20pm

Style 2   The am and pm are set with a space after the minutes:

8:40 am   11:15 am   3:00 pm   10:20 pm

Style 3   The a.m. and p.m., are set with full points and a space after the minutes:

8:40 a.m.   11:15 a.m.   3:00 p.m.   10:20 p.m.

The styles above can be used with small caps for 'am' and 'pm':

Styles   4 8:40AM   5 11:15 AM   6 10:20 P.M.

Style 7   The minutes are omitted when the time is on the hour:

8 am   3 pm

Style 8   'Noon' and 'midnight' are used for clarity:

12 noon   12 midnight

5.5.3 Order of information in dates

Rule When setting dates, only numbers are used for the days, not 1st, 2nd, 3rd, etc. unless quoting from a source in which these have been used. Set these as regular type (1st, 2nd), not superscript (1st, 2nd).

Style 1 Day first, then the month, then the year:

5 January 1982   30 April 1875   3 December 2014

Style 2 Month first, then the day followed by a comma, then the year:

January 5, 1982   April 30, 1875   December 3, 2014

5.5.4 Dates expressed in numbers

Style 1 A full point separates days, months and years:

3.11.1965   30.3.2008   13.7.1922

Style 2 A forward slash separates days, months and years:

3/11/1965   30/3/2008   13/7/1922

Style 2 The months are set in roman numerals:

3.xi.1965   30.iii.2008   13.vii.1922

5.5.5 Spans of time

Style 1 A spaced en dash indicates spans of time:

8:40 – 10:20 am   1 June – 30 September, 2010

Style 2 The word 'to' indicates spans of time:

8:40 to 10:20 am   1 June to 30 September, 2010

See 5.6 Elided numbers.

NOTES TO 5.5.4
These forms are more likely to be used in official documentation, but are not usually used in general texts, such as novels.

Be aware that in the US the order is: month, day, year.

5.6   Elided numbers

Style 1   The smallest number of digits is used, bearing in mind how the numbers are spoken:

So,   941–5   nine hundred and forty one to five

but,   911–12   nine hundred and eleven to twelve

Style 2   The smallest number of digits is used, but with a minimum of two digits after the en dash:

1941–45   368–72   22–23

Style 3   Both numbers are set in full:

1941–1945   368–372   22–23

Rule   Spans of years are not split after the first digit: 1837–945
This should be set: 1837–1945

Rule   A year which spans two calendar years, such as a financial or an academic year, is indicated by a forward slash:

2008/9   1972/3   2024/5

5.7   Roman numerals

Roman numerals may be used to number preliminary pages, chapters and volumes of multiple-volume works. They may also be used to number lists and sub-sections in documents.

Rule   Set roman numerals in capitals when used with a monarch's or pope's name:

Henry VIII   Elizabeth I   John Paul II

Rule   Set roman numerals in capitals when used as the title of a chapter or volume:

Chapter XIX   Volume V

Rule   Set roman numerals in lower case to indicate page numbers in prelims or when numbering lists:

i) Housing   ii) Transport   iii) Health   iv) Education

5.8   Spelling out numbers

Rule   Where a sentence starts with a number, it is spelled out:

to England. Twenty-eight of the men travelled back to France in

Rule   Where a sentence contains a sequence of numbers, they should all be digits or all spelled out, not a combination of both:

they were aged seven, nine, twelve and fifteen.

not:

they were aged seven, nine, 12 and 15.

Style 1   Numbers up to and including ten are spelled out.

Style 2   Numbers up to and including twelve are spelled out.

Style 3   Numbers up to and including twenty are spelled out.

Style 4   Numbers up to and including one hundred are spelled out.

Exceptions, which are never spelled out, include:

> dates
> weights and measurements
> page numbers
> figure numbers
> footnote or endnote numbers

Chapter numbers should be consistent in their numbering: all digits, all roman numerals or all spelled out.

LISTS AND TABLES

6.1 Punctuation of lists

Style 1   **List entries do not take punctuation at the end:**

View of Longwood, 1820 by Louis Marchand
The Emperor on St Helena Dictating his Memoirs to General Gourgaud
The Eylau Cemetery by Baron Gros
The Last Phase by James Sant

Style 2   **List entries take a semi-colon at the end except the final entry which takes a full point:**

View of Longwood, 1820 by Louis Marchand;
The Emperor on St Helena Dictating his Memoirs to General Gourgaud;
The Eylau Cemetery by Baron Gros;
The Last Phase by James Sant.

Style 3   **List entries take full point at the end:**

View of Longwood, 1820 by Louis Marchand.
The Emperor on St Helena Dictating his Memoirs to General Gourgaud.
The Eylau Cemetery by Baron Gros.
The Last Phase by James Sant.

6.2 Layout of lists

Style 1   **Entries separated by space:**

View of Longwood, 1820 by Louis Marchand (p.39). Courtesy of Réunion des Musées Nationaux

The Emperor on St Helena Dictating his Memoirs to General Gourgaud (p.82). A lithograph by Lanzedelly after a painting by Carl August von Steuben. From the collection Archiv für Kunst und Geschichte, Berlin (AKG, London)

The Eylau Cemetery by Baron Gros (p.102). Courtesy of Daniel Arnaudet

NOTE TO 6.1
For punctuation of lists in continuous text, see 3.2.1.

Style 2   The first lines of entries hang out to the left:

> View of Longwood, 1820 by Louis Marchand (p.39). Courtesy of Réunion des Musées Nationaux
> The Emperor on St Helena Dictating his Memoirs to General Gourgaud (p.82). A lithograph by Lanzedelly after a painting by Carl August von Steuben. From the collection Archiv für Kunst und Geschichte, Berlin (AKG, London)
> The Eylau Cemetery by Baron Gros (p.102). Courtesy of Daniel Arnaudet

Style 3   Entries indicated by a bullet point or some other symbol:

- View of Longwood, 1820 by Louis Marchand (p.39). Courtesy of Réunion des Musées Nationaux
- The Emperor on St Helena Dictating his Memoirs to General Gourgaud (p.82). A lithograph by Lanzedelly after a painting by Carl August von Steuben. From the collection Archiv für Kunst und Geschichte, Berlin (AKG, London)
- The Eylau Cemetery by Baron Gros (p.102). Courtesy of Daniel Arnaudet

6.3   Numbered lists

Style 1   Numbers are hung out to the left, and ranged right against the text which is ranged left:

> 98   View of Longwood, 1820 by Louis Marchand
> 99   The Emperor on St Helena Dictating his Memoirs to General Gourgaud
> 100 The Eylau Cemetery by Baron Gros
> 101 The Last Phase by James Sant

Style 2   Numbers hung out to the left, and ranged left. The text is also ranged left:

> 98   View of Longwood, 1820 by Louis Marchand
> 99   The Emperor on St Helena Dictating his Memoirs to General Gourgaud
> 100 The Eylau Cemetery by Baron Gros
> 101 The Last Phase by James Sant

Style 3 overleaf

Numbers are followed by a full point. There is space between entries:

98. *View of Longwood, 1820* by Louis Marchand (p.39). Courtesy of Réunion des Musées Nationaux.

99. *The Emperor on St Helena Dictating his Memoirs to General Gourgaud* (p.82). A lithograph by Lanzedelly after a painting by Carl August von Steuben. From the collection Archiv für Kunst und Geschichte, Berlin (AKG, London).

100. *The Eylau Cemetery* by Baron Gros (p.102). Courtesy of Daniel Arnaudet.

6.4 Format and position of tables

6.4.1 *Table orientation*

Style 1 Tables – whether placed within the text or on a separate page – are placed the same way up as the main text.

Style 2 Tables which appear on pages by themselves may be rotated 90° anti-clockwise on the page allowing the table to be reproduced at a larger size. The reader rotates the book 90° clockwise.

6.4.2 *Column width in tables*

Column width is determined by content, whilst maintaining consistency where possible. In the example below, the two columns on the left are the same width and the three columns on the right are the same width:

date BC	zone	climate phase	climate	vegetation
14,000	Ia	Oldest Dryas	cold	tundra
	Ib	Boiling interstadial	warmer	
	Ic	Older Dryas	readvances of ice	
12,000	II	Allerod interstadial	warmer	birch woodland
10,000	III	Younger Dryas		tundra

6.4.3 *Position of tables within the text*

Style 1   Tables are placed as close as possible to, but always after, their mention in the text.

Style 2   Tables are placed together as an appendix at the end of the text.

6.4.4 *Extensive tables*

When a table runs onto a second page, the column widths are the same on both pages. The rule at the foot of the table on the first page is omitted to show the table has not finished. The headings are repeated on the second page.

6.5 Typography within tables

6.5.1 *Type size of tables*

Style 1   Text within the table is set smaller than the main text of the publication.

Style 2   Text within the table is set at the same size as the main text of the publication.

6.5.2 *Longer entries*

Style 1   Where the text of an entry goes onto a second or third line, these lines are indented. In this example there is space between entries:

Increase of alder (Mesolithic)

Early Neolithic forest clearance – elm decline (first farmers *c.*1500 BC)

Increase of ash and birch (late Neolithic – early Bronze Age)

Increase of ash, birch, hornbeam and beech; decline of lime (middle and late Bronze Age)

Style 2 overleaf

Style 2 Where the text of an entry goes onto a second or third line, these lines are not indented. There is space between entries:

Increase of alder (Mesolithic)

Early Neolithic forest clearance – elm decline (first farmers c.1500 BC)

Increase of ash and birch (late Neolithic – early Bronze Age)

Increase of ash, birch, hornbeam and beech; decline of lime (middle and late Bronze Age)

Birch and beech more prominent (Iron Age)

6.5.3   Headings within tables

Style 1 Titles within a table are indicated by use of bold font:

date	zone	climate phase	climate	vegetation
14,000	Ia	Oldest Dryas	cold	tundra
	Ib	Boiling interstadial	warmer	
	Ic	Older Dryas	readvances of ice	
12,000	II	Allerod interstadial	warmer	birch woodland
10,000	III	Younger Dryas		tundra

Style 2 Titles within a table are indicated by use of a second colour:

date	zone	climate phase	climate	vegetation
14,000	Ia	Oldest Dryas	cold	tundra
	Ib	Boiling interstadial	warmer	
	Ic	Older Dryas	readvances of ice	
12,000	II	Allerod interstadial	warmer	birch woodland
10,000	III	Younger Dryas		tundra

Style 3   Titles within a table are indicated by use of capitals or small caps:

DATE	ZONE	CLIMATE PHASE	CLIMATE	VEGETATION
14,000	Ia	Oldest Dryas	cold	tundra
	Ib	Boiling interstadial	warmer	
	Ic	Older Dryas	readvances of ice	
12,000	II	Allerod interstadial	warmer	birch woodland
10,000	III	Younger Dryas		tundra

Style 4   Titles within a table are indicated by use of a different font:

date	zone	climate phase	climate	vegetation
14,000	Ia	Oldest Dryas	cold	tundra
	Ib	Boiling interstadial	warmer	
	Ic	Older Dryas	readvances of ice	
12,000	II	Allerod interstadial	warmer	birch woodland
10,000	III	Younger Dryas		tundra

NOTES TO 6.5.3

While entries and headings in tables are usually set ranged left, the headings can be set to a different alignment if they are longer than the entries. See the 'zone' column in the above tables.

Style 2: using colour will add substantially to the cost of printing, so this should only be done in publications that are already in four-colour.

Style 3: caps and small caps take up more space, so this is not appropriate for tables with long headings.

6.6   Use of rules in tables

Style 1   Use the minimum number of rules necessary to make the meaning of the table clear:

DATE	SYSTEM	CLASS	TYPE
-200	Learned Chinese	C	1
-180	Hebraic alphabetic	A	3
-150	Nabataean	B	1
+100	Khatraean	B	1
+100	Palmyrenean	B	1
+270	Coptic alphabetic (Egypt)	A	3
+292	Maya (long form of dates)	B	5

Style 2   Use a border to define the outside of the table and the minimum number of rules inside:

DATE	SYSTEM	CLASS	TYPE
-200	Learned Chinese	C	1
-180	Hebraic alphabetic	A	3
-150	Nabataean	B	1
+100	Khatraean	B	1
+100	Palmyrenean	B	1
+270	Coptic alphabetic (Egypt)	A	3
+292	Maya (long form of dates)	B	5

Style 3   Use a border to define the outside of the table and a lighter weight of rule to define the entries inside the table:

DATE	SYSTEM	CLASS	TYPE
-200	Learned Chinese	C	1
-180	Hebraic alphabetic	A	3
-150	Nabataean	B	1
+100	Khatraean	B	1
+100	Palmyrenean	B	1
+270	Coptic alphabetic (Egypt)	A	3

Style 4 Use alternate tinted blocks to distinguish the entries within the table:

DATE	SYSTEM	CLASS	TYPE
-200	Learned Chinese	C	1
-180	Hebraic alphabetic	A	3
-150	Nabataean	B	1
+100	Khatraean	B	1
+100	Palmyrenean	B	1
+270	Coptic alphabetic (Egypt)	A	3

NOTES TO 6.6

0.25pt rule

0.5pt rule

0.75pt rule

1pt rule

1.5pt rule

5% tint of black

10% tint of black

15% tint of black

20% tint of black

25% tint of black

Please note that printing results can vary, so the tones shown above are approximate.

6.7   Chronologies (time lines)

Events for each year are listed chronologically, separated by full points:

	Gillray's Life	Home Affairs	International Affairs
1784	Publishes *Love in a Coffin*, 30 December.	Dissolution of Parliament. Fox re-elected for constituency of Westminster in the March General Election. Pitt is made Prime Minister.	
1785		George, Prince of Wales, marries Mrs Fitzherbert.	In Paris, Jacques-Louis David exhibits *Oath of the Horatii*.
1786	Resumes satirical work. Published by William Holland and Samuel Fores.	Edmund Burke introduces an impeachment process against Warren Hastings of the East India Company.	
1787	Publishes *Ancient Music*, 10 May, and *Monstrous Craws*, 29 May.		Anglo-French commercial treaty.

The width of columns will depend on the length of the entries. In the above example there is more text in the Home Affairs column so that column is slightly wider.

6.8 Numbers in tables

6.8.1 *Lining and non-lining figures in tables*

An important feature of lining figures is that each digit is set to the same width, so when placed in columns they align vertically. This makes lining figures a better choice for setting tables. Some typefaces have a special *tab font* for this use.

Style 1 Lining figures are used in tables, regardless of whether they are used in the main text:

2,682	458	4,294
4,297	663	587
557	1,586	933
496	5,071	692
485	428	1,058
691	221	184

Style 2 Lining or non-lining figures are used in tables, to match the font used in the main text. The non-lining figures do not align vertically:

2,682	458	4,294
4,297	663	587
557	1,586	933
496	5,071	692
485	428	1,058
691	221	184

6.8.2 *Typography in financial reports*

In financial reports negative amounts are indicated by placing round brackets around the numbers and nil amounts shown by a dash ranged right. Totals are in a bold font:

2,682	(458)	4,294
–	–	(587)
557	1,586	933
496	5,071	–
3,735	**6,199**	**4,640**

HEADINGS AND SUB-HEADINGS

INTRODUCTION TO HEADINGS AND SUB-HEADINGS

A publication can be divided up in many different ways. The following are the most common:

part – the largest division of the text. Usually indicated by a page called a *part-title* containing the number and title of the part.
chapter – usually each chapter starts on a new page and is numbered or titled or both.
sub-chapter – there may be multiple levels of these.

7.1   Pagination of parts and chapters

A part is indicated by a full-page or double-page part-title. The part may be further sub-divided into chapters.

Style 1   Part-title on recto, followed by blank verso, followed by main text on recto.

Style 2   Part-title on recto, followed by main text on verso.

Style 3   Part-title on double-page spread, followed by blank verso, followed by main text on recto.

Style 4   Part-title on double-page spread, followed by main text on verso.

7.2   Chapters and sub-chapters

7.2.1   *New chapters*

Style 1   Each chapter starts on a new page (opposite page, left). The text starts down the page, usually between a quarter and half way down. This *chapter drop* is consistent throughout the publication and may contain a chapter number, a chapter heading, or both.

NOTES TO 7.2.1

Style 1: the last page of each chapter should contain no fewer than four lines of text.

Style 2 is appropriate only when there are short chapters, not divided into sub-chapters, and when space is limited.

Style 2 Each chapter starts beneath the previous chapter (it is *run-on*). The chapters are separated by space and a number or title.

If a new chapter falls at the foot of a page with fewer than three lines of text below the heading, leave a space and start the chapter at the top of the next page.

There should not be only one or two lines of text above a chapter heading at the top of a page. Manipulate the text to take the lines back, or push lines forward.

Style 1

Style 2

7.2.2   *Recto/verso starts*

Style 1 Each chapter starts as it falls, either on a recto or a verso.

Style 2 Each chapter starts on a recto, leaving the preceding verso blank if necessary.

Style 3 Start each chapter on a verso, but do not leave the preceding recto blank.

It is difficult to maintain this arrangement of text, without blank rectos, but in an illustrated publication there may be more possibilities to push text forward or back so that each chapter ends on a recto.

A variation of this style is to start each chapter with a full-page image on the verso and the chapter text starting on the opposite recto.

NOTE TO 7.2.2

Style 2 is more appropriate when the text is divided into separate entities, such as short stories or essays.

The table opposite shows how a text can be sub-divided into sections with different levels of heading, known as the *heading hierarchy*.

Style 1   Each chapter starts on a new page with sub-chapters run on. Each level of heading is set in a different style, from within the same font family, reflecting its position in the hierarchy.

Style 2   Chapters and sub-chapters are numbered using the following system:

1	Chapter heading
1.1	A-heading
1.1.1	B-heading
1.1.1 a	C-heading

Headings from the table opposite would be numbered as follows:

4	Industry	4.1.4	Hemp
4.1	Textiles	4.1.5	Silk
4.1.1	Wool	4.1.6	Needlecraft
4.1.2	Cotton	4.1.6 a	Knitting
4.1.2 a	Looms	4.1.6 b	Lace
4.1.2 b	Power-looms	4.2	Leather
4.1.3	Flax & Linen	4.3	Pottery

Rule   There is a space of at least one line between sub-sections:

There are many old mills in the southeast Lancashire–south Derbyshire complex, and indeed the industrial landscape is worth studying.

4.1.3 Flax & Linen

Flax was used widely in the ancient world, from Neolithic times on, as a textile source. At first its tough stems were used in many

CHAPTER TITLE: **INDUSTRY**

A-HEADINGS	B-headings	*C-headings*

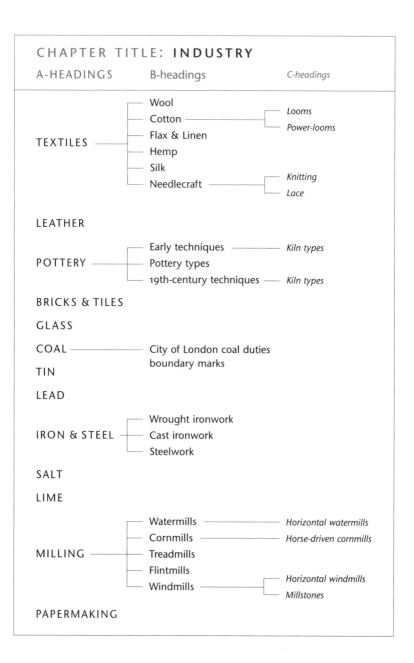

TEXTILES
- Wool
- Cotton
  - *Looms*
  - *Power-looms*
- Flax & Linen
- Hemp
- Silk
- Needlecraft
  - *Knitting*
  - *Lace*

LEATHER

POTTERY
- Early techniques — *Kiln types*
- Pottery types
- 19th-century techniques — *Kiln types*

BRICKS & TILES

GLASS

COAL — City of London coal duties boundary marks

TIN

LEAD

IRON & STEEL
- Wrought ironwork
- Cast ironwork
- Steelwork

SALT

LIME

MILLING
- Watermills — *Horizontal watermills*
- Cornmills — *Horse-driven cornmills*
- Treadmills
- Flintmills
- Windmills
  - *Horizontal windmills*
  - *Millstones*

PAPERMAKING

7.3 Chapter headings

The following sections serve as a basis from which the designer can formulate a design within the house style of the publisher. They do not contain every possibility for the styling of headings and sub-headings.

7.3.1 *Type style of chapter headings*

Style 1 Chapter headings are set in the same font as the body text, at a larger size:

A Day in the Country

Style 2 Chapter headings are set in the same font as the body text, at a larger size and in capitals. These should be letterspaced for improved legibility:

A DAY IN THE COUNTRY

Style 3 Chapter headings are set in the same font as the body text, at a larger size and in italic:

A Day in the Country

Style 4 Chapter headings are set in the same font as the body text, at a larger size and in a heavier weight:

A Day in the Country

Style 5 Chapter headings are set in a display font, distinct from the body text:

A Day in the Country

Style 1   Chapter headings are set ranged left in the text panel:

A Day in the Country

Though their first film together was at best a flop and may not even have been released, Tati and his friend Rhum managed to find an

Style 2   Chapter headings are set centred in the text panel:

A Day in the Country

Though their first film together was at best a flop and may not even have been released, Tati and his friend Rhum managed to find an

Style 3   Chapter headings are set ranged right in the text panel:

A Day in the Country

Though their first film together was at best a flop and may not even have been released, Tati and his friend Rhum managed to find an

Style 4   Chapter headings are set indented in the text panel:

A Day in the Country

Though their first film together was at best a flop and may not even have been released, Tati and his friend Rhum managed to find an

Style 5   Chapter headings are hung out of the text panel:

A Day in the Country

Though their first film together was at best a flop and may not even have been released, Tati and his friend Rhum managed to find an

7.3.3 Vertical position of chapter headings

Style 1 Chapter headings are set at the top of the text panel with a drop to the start of the body text.

Style 2 Chapter headings are set midway between the top of the text panel and the start of the body text.

Style 3 Chapter headings are set close to the start of the body text.

Style 1

Style 2

Style 3

7.3.4   *Chapter numbers*

Style 1   Chapter numbers are set in Arabic numerals:

12

Style 2   Chapter numbers are set in roman numerals:

XII

Style 3   Chapter numbers are set spelled out:

Twelve

Style 4   Chapter numbers are set in Arabic numerals with the word 'chapter':

Chapter 12

Style 5   Set chapter numbers in roman numerals with the word 'chapter':

CHAPTER XII

Style 6   Chapter numbers are set spelled out with the word 'chapter':

Chapter Twelve

7.3.5   *Combining chapter numbers and chapter titles*

Style 1   Chapter numbers are set on the same line as the chapter title:

12 A Day in the Country

Style 2   Chapter numbers are set on the line above the chapter title:

CHAPTER 12

A Day in the Country

7.4	Sub-headings
7.4.1	*Type style of sub-headings*
Rule	Different levels of sub-headings should be set using fonts from the same typeface family, e.g. italics, capitals, small caps.
Style 1	The same font family is used for sub-headings as for the body text. The sample below is in Albertina:

Religious architecture A-heading

EARLY ENGLISH STYLE B-heading

The Church in the Middle Ages C-heading

The early Middle Ages was a period of major construction, which produced many of our finest cathedrals, such as Canterbury, Wells, Lincoln and Salisbury, and great monastic churches, like Hexham

Style 2	A display font is used for sub-headings, ensuring that it has the necessary range of styles. The sample below has sub-headings in Rialto roman, small caps and italic with body text in Albertina:

Religious architecture A-heading

EARLY ENGLISH STYLE B-heading

The Church in the Middle Ages C-heading

The early Middle Ages was a period of major construction, which produced many of our finest cathedrals, such as Canterbury, Wells, Lincoln and Salisbury, and great monastic churches, like Hexham

Rule   Sub-headings that are higher in the hierarchy should be visually larger than lower headings. Bear in mind that capitals look larger than lower-case and that heavier fonts can look larger than lighter fonts. Decisions on sizes should be made using visual judgement, and not a formula based on type sizes. See also 7.4.5 *Combining different levels of headings*.

Religious architecture   A-heading

EARLY ENGLISH STYLE   B-heading

The Church in the Middle Ages   C-heading

The monastic buildings   D-heading

THE CLOISTERS   E-heading

Floor tiles   F-heading

The early Middle Ages was a period of major construction, which produced many of our finest cathedrals, such as Canterbury, Wells, Lincoln and Salisbury, and great monastic churches, like Hexham

The example above is extensive, with six levels of sub-heading. In these cases start with the lowest level of heading, making it just larger than the body text, and work up from there. Bear in mind:

frequency – which is the most frequently used level of heading? Use the most legible type style for this.

length of headings – find the longest and shortest headings and make sure the size of both looks comfortable.

Style 1   Sub-headings are ranged left in the text panel. This is the preferred setting if the chapter headings are ranged left:

EARLY ENGLISH STYLE

The Church in the Middle Ages

The early Middle Ages was a period of major construction, which produced many of our finest cathedrals, such as Canterbury, Wells,

Style 2   Sub-headings are centred in the text panel. This is the preferred style if the chapter headings are centred:

EARLY ENGLISH STYLE

The Church in the Middle Ages

The early Middle Ages was a period of major construction, which produced many of our finest cathedrals, such as Canterbury, Wells,

Style 3   A combination of ranged left and centred sub-headings is used:

EARLY ENGLISH STYLE

The Church in the Middle Ages

The early Middle Ages was a period of major construction, which produced many of our finest cathedrals, such as Canterbury, Wells,

Rule   If combining ranged left and centred sub-headings, centred setting is used for sub-headings further up the hierarchy and ranged left setting is used for lower-level headings.

Rule   Sub-headings are set closer to the text below than to the text above.

Rule   The higher up the hierarchy, the greater the space between sub-sections.

Style 1   Three line-spaces are used above the sub-heading, one below:

being designed not just for its own aesthetic effect but also as a supporting framework for lively, colourful stained glass.

3#

Composite columns

1#

Composite pier and columns seem to have developed as a result of the wish to provide a clear visual connection between elaborately

Style 2   Two line-spaces are used above the sub-heading, one below:

being designed not just for its own aesthetic effect but also as a supporting framework for lively, colourful stained glass.

2#

Composite columns

1#

Composite pier and columns seem to have developed as a result of the wish to provide a clear visual connection between elaborately

Style 3   One-and-a-half line-spaces are used above the sub-heading, half
          below:

          being designed not just for its own aesthetic effect but also as a
          supporting framework for lively, colourful stained glass.

1½ #

          COMPOSITE COLUMNS
½ #
          Composite pier and columns seem to have developed as a result of
          the wish to provide a clear visual connection between elaborately

Style 4   One line-space is used above the sub-heading, none below:

          being designed not just for its own aesthetic effect but also as a
          supporting framework for lively, colourful stained glass.

1 #

          Composite columns
          Composite pier and columns seem to have developed as a result of
          the wish to provide a clear visual connection between elaborately

---

7.4.5   *Combining different levels of headings*

Rule   Where two or more headings appear together, keeping the space
          before and after each heading will result in a gappy page. Adjust
          the vertical spacing visually, bearing in mind the following points:

          The body text should stay aligned to the baseline grid (see opposite).

          The treatment for each combination of headings should be consistent
          throughout the publication.

          Space between lower, smaller headings should be less than space
          between higher, larger headings.

The monastic buildings

THE CLOISTERS
Floor plan

The name cloister means simply an enclosed space (Latin *claustrum*), but it has come to refer not just to the open ground in the middle

EARLY ENGLISH STYLE

The Church in the Middle Ages

The early Middle Ages was a period of major construction, which produced many of our finest cathedrals, such as Canterbury, Wells,

Parish churches

CHURCH FURNISHINGS
Furnishings of the choir

Little remains of the special furnishings which were provided in the choir of cathedrals and abbey churches, and those which survive

7.5 Alternative type styles at the start of a chapter

The following styles may be used in conjunction with a chapter title or where chapters do not have a title. They are not usually used with sub-headings.

7.5.1 *Drop caps at the start of a chapter*

Style 1 **The first character of a chapter is set as a drop cap:**

T he early Middle Ages was a period of major construction, which produced many of our finest cathedrals, such as Wells, Lincoln and Salisbury, and great monastic churches, like Hexham

If the opening sentence starts with a quotation mark, include this, dropping two characters, preferably hanging out the quotation mark:

'T he early Middle Ages was a period of major construction, which produced many of our finest cathedrals, such as Wells,

7.5.2 *Small caps at the start of a chapter*

Style 1 **The first line of a chapter is set in letterspaced small caps:**

THE EARLY MIDDLE AGES WAS A PERIOD OF MAJOR construction, which produced many of our finest cathedrals, such as Wells, Lincoln and Salisbury, and great monastic churches, like

Style 2 **The first four words of a chapter are set in letterspaced small caps:**

THE EARLY MIDDLE AGES was a period of major construction, which produced many of our finest cathedrals, such as Wells, Lincoln and Salisbury, and great monastic churches, like Hexham

NOTES TO 7.5.1

The styles suggested in 7.5.1 and 7.5.2 may be combined.

Drop caps may be three or more lines deep. Care should be taken over the spacing between the drop cap and body text.

7.6 Epigraphs at the start of a chapter

A chapter epigraph is placed below the chapter number and heading, if there is one. Text is about the same size as the body text: it can be slightly larger or smaller. There are many different ways of styling the text. The examples given below may be used as a starting point.

Style 1   The epigraph is centred, if a single line, and indented if multiple lines. Type style is italic with the author in small caps:

Chapter 16

Let all be set forth so that all may be healed.
ÉMILE ZOLA

Style 2   As Style 1, but with the epigraph in roman:

Chapter 16

Let all be set forth so that all may be healed.
ÉMILE ZOLA

Style 3   As Style 1 or 2, but with the author ranged right:

Chapter 16

Let all be set forth so that all may be healed.
ÉMILE ZOLA

7.7 Running heads and running feet

7.7.1 *Placement of running heads*

Style 1 **Running heads are placed above the text panel, set centred:**

ARCHITECTURE IN BRITAIN

there had been mural fireplaces in more important buildings since Norman times, halls with central fireplaces continued to be built

Style 2 **Running heads are placed above the text panel, aligned with the outside edge of the text panel:**

ARCHITECTURE IN BRITAIN

there had been mural fireplaces in more important buildings since Norman times, halls with central fireplaces continued to be built

Rule **The running head is omitted from the first page of a new chapter (unless chapters are run-on). Running heads and feet do not appear on blank pages or preliminary pages and can be omitted from pages containing only an illustration.**

7.7.2 *Type style of running heads*

Style 1 **Running heads are set in letterspaced small caps:**

ARCHITECTURE IN BRITAIN

there had been mural fireplaces in more important buildings since Norman times, halls with central fireplaces continued to be built

Style 2 **Running heads are set in italics:**

Architecture in Britain

there had been mural fireplaces in more important buildings since Norman times, halls with central fireplaces continued to be built

7.7.3   Content of running heads

Style 1   verso: author name   recto: book title

LUCY ARCHER

size of the great hall of a medieval house, rising the full height
of the building, made it necessary to have an open truss about

ARCHITECTURE IN BRITAIN

there had been mural fireplaces in more important buildings since
Norman times, halls with central fireplaces continued to be built

Style 2   verso: book title   recto: chapter title

ARCHITECTURE IN BRITAIN

size of the great hall of a medieval house, rising the full height
of the building, made it necessary to have an open truss about

THE MEDIEVAL PERIOD

there had been mural fireplaces in more important buildings since
Norman times, halls with central fireplaces continued to be built

Style 3   verso: chapter title   recto: sub-chapter title

THE MEDIEVAL PERIOD

size of the great hall of a medieval house, rising the full height
of the building, made it necessary to have an open truss about

ROOFS OF GREAT HALLS

there had been mural fireplaces in more important buildings since
Norman times, halls with central fireplaces continued to be built

Style 4   The running head of each page describes the content on that page.
This is done in consultation with the author.

7.7.4 Running heads in reference works

In reference books that are organised alphabetically, the running heads may be used to direct readers around the text.

Style 1 Whole words are used in the running heads, separated by an en dash:

LARDER–LASSO   LAST–LATTER   LAUD–LAWN

Style 2 Whole words are used in the running heads, separated by a vertical dash:

LARDER | LASSO   LAST | LATTER   LAUD | LAWN

Style 3 Abbreviated forms are used in the running heads. The length of these will vary depending on the words. They are separated by an en dash:

LAR–LASS   LAST–LAT   LAU–LAW

7.7.5 Running heads and rules

Style 1 A printed rule may be placed between running head and main text:

ARCHITECTURE IN BRITAIN

---

there had been mural fireplaces in more important buildings since Norman times, halls with central fireplaces continued to be built

---

7.7.6 Running feet

Running feet are placed at the foot of the page, below the text panel, ranged to the fore-edge:

it was also significant for his literary career. And there is no question, although the degree is hard to assess, that through

118 CAMBRIDGE

For type style and content, the Styles for running heads can be used.

In large-format books with wider margins, the fore-edge margin may be used for this purpose.

7.8 Folios (page numbers)

Folios should be placed consistently throughout a publication. Placement is a matter for the designer, but in books without running heads, the most common positions are:

Style 1 Beneath the text panel, set centred:

career. And there is no question, although the degree is hard to

116

Style 2 Beneath the text panel, aligned with the outer edge of the text:

career. And there is no question, although the degree is hard to

117

Style 3 In books with running heads, the folios may be set on the same line as the centred running head:

116   CAMBRIDGE

was also significant for his literary career. And there is no question, although the degree is hard to assess, that through friendship with

Style 4 Or with both elements aligned to the outer edge of the text panel:

CAMBRIDGE   113

was also significant for his literary career. And there is no question, although the degree is hard to assess, that through friendship with

Style 5 Or with both elements centred:

118 CAMBRIDGE

was also significant for his literary career. And there is no question, although the degree is hard to assess, that through friendship with

Rule Folios are not placed on blank pages or on prelims before and including the contents page.

ILLUSTRATIONS AND CAPTIONS

Introduction to using illustrations, 116

INTRODUCTION TO USING ILLUSTRATIONS

Although illustrations do not form a part of typography, designers and editors will have to deal with them whether in the simplest leaflet or the most complex illustrated book. An understanding of the use of illustrations is essential; from gaining permissions for their use to ensuring that they are of sufficient quality.

Illustrations can include:

> Four-colour photographs
> Four-colour images of works of art
> Black-and-white photographs
> Drawings in colour or black and white with shading
> Line drawings
> Maps
> Charts
> Pie charts
> Graphs
> Genealogical charts
> Decorative elements

All these are referred to as *artwork*. They add to the text by expanding the reader's understanding. In children's books or graphic novels they make up a large proportion of the publication.

Artwork is supplied in a digital form, from digital cameras, image creation programs such as Adobe Illustrator® or by scanning the originals.

In magazines, brochures, posters and leaflets they may be the major feature of a design and the texts are laid out around the illustrations.

Copyright permissions must be obtained from the institutions, artists or photographers, or their agents, for the use any illustration even if they have been used in previous publications.

Reproduction rights of works of art held in institutions are jealously guarded and subject to a reproduction charge. Permissions need to be cleared well in advance of publication and charges may be related to the number of copies to be printed. A specific mention of the copyright holders in the publication is routinely part of the permission.

Some institutions offer images of art works *in the public domain*. These are free of reproduction fees but should be attributed to the institution.

If the whole of the image is not used, it is *cropped*. It may be necessary to get the copyright holder's pemission for this, especially for works of art.

Care should be taken in using illustrations sourced from the web – frequently they are not of a high enough resolution for print use. If it is possible to use them for print, permissions may nevertheless be required.

Placing images in the layout

There are two basic layout treatments for illustrations:

integrated images – the images are placed within the text as close to their mention in the text as possible.

plate sections – all the images are grouped in a separately printed section, often on a coated paper to improve the quality of reproduction. These are inserted within the other sections when the whole is bound. Picture captions are placed within the plate section.

Full-page illustrations and double-page spread illustrations can be used in both these layout treatments.

The layout of illustrations in magazines and brochures is less rigid; the emphasis is on impact and drawing the attention of the reader.

Colour

Placing four-colour illustrations scattered throughout a book with predominently black text pages is expensive: four-colour printing plates have to be run for every section containing a colour image. Plate sections reduce this cost.

Image resolution for printing

The resolution of an image has to be at least 300 dpi to print satisfactorily. This is dealt with in *Appendix D.*

Integrated illustrations

Integrated illustrations may be placed within the text panel, outside the text panel or *bled-out*.

Placed within the text panel:

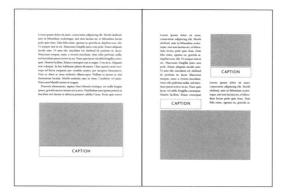

Placed both inside and outside the text panel:

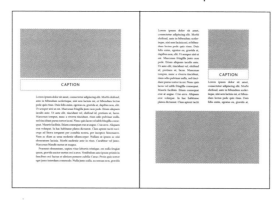

The required position for an integrated image should be marked by the editor in the text document by a coloured tag:

the bridge on the far left of the river [Figure 4.5]. He walked over to

These may be removed after the layout or retained to aid the reader if required:

the bridge on the far left of the river (Fig. 4.5). He walked over to

Bled-out illustrations

An illustration that is to go to the trimmed edge of a page is *bled-out*. The image is printed at a larger size than the printed page so when the page is trimmed no white areas remain. An image used in this way loses at least 3 mm on the trimmed edges.

Take care that there is sufficient image to avoid important areas being lost as in the example on the right:

A bled-out illustration may occupy a full page or a portion of it:

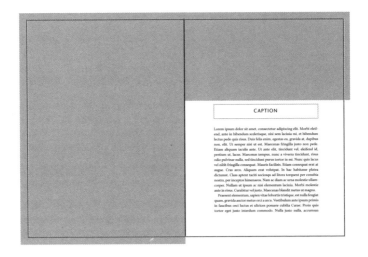

8.1 Illustrations

8.1.1 *Labelling illustrations*

Diagrams, plans, maps, graphs and charts may require explanatory labels. These should be supplied as part of the artwork bearing in mind the size of reproduction. The type style of the labels should be sympathetic to the typography in the rest of the publication.

If placing the label within the drawing obscures any areas a *leader line* is used to indicate the feature. Arrow heads are unnecessary.

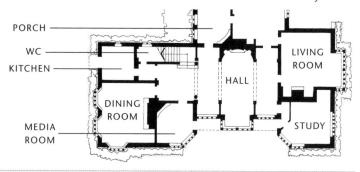

8.1.2 *Keys*

Keys explain details used in maps, diagrams, plans, graphs and charts:

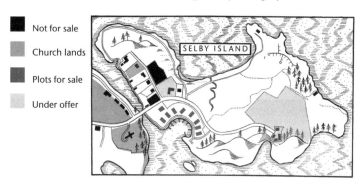

If colour is not available, a sequence of grey shades or dots can be used:

8.1.3 *How images can go wrong*

Graphs and other drawn artworks must be created bearing in mind that they may be subject to reduction. Reduced fine lines and text may appear too faint in print.

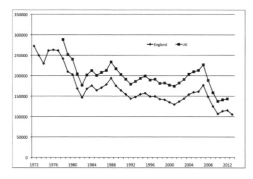

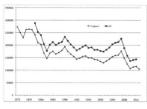

The reduced lines become too faint.

Four-colour scans are screened to provide dots for each of the CMYK's coloured inks for printing (see *Appendix D*). If scans are made from previously printed material, the second screening produces unacceptable patterns (a *moiré*). The printer's repro department may be able to help to reduce this effect.

The same *moiré* effect can occur with artwork that contains finely drawn lines close together. The only way to check this before printing is with a costly wet-proof. When reproducing images of this kind, discuss the potential problems with the printer at the earliest opportunity to ensure that the output files are produced correctly.

Proofs made using laser or bubble-jet printing do not produce an accurate reproduction of sharpness or colour values. They are used only to check text, picture position and pagination. Do not rely on these for evidence of final print quality especially of illustrated work. See *Appendix A*.

The profile used to create a PDF of an illustration may not be of print quality. The provider may be unaware of the profile or be unable to confirm that it is of print quality. Getting a high-resolution proof made before printing is the only way of confirming the quality.

8.2 Captions

8.2.1 *Type size and style of captions relative to body text*

Style 1   Captions are set at 2 pt smaller than the body text:

to enter the Royal College of Art's competition for digital   10 pt

Above: The digital representation shown from the right   8 pt

Style 2   Captions are set at the same size as the body text:

to enter the Royal College of Art's competition for digital   10 pt

Above: The digital representation shown from the right   10 pt

8.2.2 *Typeface choices for captions*

Style 1   Captions are set in same typeface as body text with italics for titles:

Jean Watteau (1684–1721), *Les Noces.* Sir John Soane's Museum

Style 2   Captions are set in italic with opposite font for titles:

Jean Watteau (1684–1721), Les Noces. Sir John Soane's Museum

Style 3   Captions are set different typeface, for example a sans-serif, with italics for titles:

Jean Watteau (1684–1721), *Les Noces.* Sir John Soane's Museum

NOTES TO 8.2.1
Style 1 is the standard format.

Style 2 is for books where captions are extensive and constitute a significant part of the text. Care needs to be taken to distinguish between caption and text.

NOTES TO 8.2.1 AND 8.2.2
The editor should decide whether to place credits including photographers, copyright owners of illustrations or institutions in each caption or within a list of picure credits as endmatter.

8.2.3　*Position of captions*

Style 1　**Captions centred**　　Style 2　**Captions ranged left**

Jean Watteau, *Les Noces*　　Jean Watteau, *Les Noces*

In both styles the space between the base of the illustration and the caption should be consistent.

Style 2 is preferable if the body text layout is ranged left.

8.2.4　*Punctuation of captions*

Style 1　**Captions do not take a full point at the end:**

View from the ground floor　　The mansion's front door
hall towards the new kitchen

Style 2　**Captions do take a full point at the end:**

View from the ground floor　　The mansion's front door.
hall towards the new kitchen.

Style 3　**Caption takes a full point at the end only if it consists of a complete sentence. Incomplete sentences do not take a full point:**

The hall's fanlight is restored to its original position.

The mansion's front door

8.2.5 Numbering captions

Style 1 Captions are numbered using numerals only:

78 View from the ground floor towards the new hall

Style 2 Captions are numbered using Fig. or Pl. followed by the numeral:

Fig. 78 View from the ground floor towards the new hall

Style 3 Captions are numbered using Fig. or Pl. followed by the numeral and a full point:

Fig. 78. View from the ground floor towards the new hall

The use of the word 'Figure' or 'Plate' is an editorial choice; the latter is less common now. They are abbreviated to Fig. or Pl. (Figs or Pls, plural) followed by the number.

8.2.6 Extensive captions

Set to either side of the illustration:

Háfíz of Shíráz: This magnificent work was bought by Henry E. Huntington, a man who had made his fortune in the railroad industry and over the course of his lifetime created one of the most important libraries in the world at his ranch in San Marino, Pasadena.

The text for extensive captions set in a narrow measure is more easily read if set ranged left. The type size is set to match caption style throughout the book.

Separate each caption clearly with a space after. Indications of the positions are noted in a clockwise direction from the top left; these are italicised, followed by a colon. Keep consistent throughout the book.

Fig. 21. *Top left*: John Addington – *Wine, Women, and Song.* John Stonehouse.

Fig. 22. *Top right*: Work done on the Bible given to President Roosevelt.

Fig. 23. *Bottom right*: Háfiz of Shíráz: This work was bought by Henry E. Huntington, a man who had made his fortune in the railroad industry.

Fig. 24. *Bottom left*: Thomas Carlyle; *The French Revolution.* Executed by George Sutcliffe.

'Tombstone' captions for art catalogues

This refers to a list of technical, bibliographical and provenance details that appear in a catalogue entry. Details of entries will vary. In the examples below the sequence is: catalogue number; artist and dates; title of artwork; holding institution; date of painting; size of the object and materials. The editor will decide the relative importance to be given to each item. There are many ways of designing these entries; the following serve as a starting point:

Style 1 The same typeface and size is used for all the elements:

28. Joshua Reynolds (1723–1792)
The 4th Duke of Queensberry (Old Q) as Earl of March
The Wallace Collection
1759
98.8 × 71.3 cm
Oil on canvas

Style 2 A larger size is used for the number, artist and title, and smaller size is used for the other details:

28. Joshua Reynolds (1723–1792)
The 4th Duke of Queensberry (Old Q) as Earl of March

The Wallace Collection
1759
98.8 × 71.3 cm
Oil on canvas

Style 3 A different font is used, usually a sans-serif for the details:

28. Joshua Reynolds (1723–1792)
The 4th Duke of Queensberry (Old Q) as Earl of March

The Wallace Collection
1759
98.8 × 71.3 cm
Oil on canvas

8.2.9 Captions in the side margins

These are captions set to the side of the main text panel referring to an illustration placed within the main text panel. They are usually positioned in the fore-edge margin; the top of the caption to align with the top of the illustration.

The type style follows the caption style chosen for the book. The format and layout of the page requires wide margins to accommodate the caption.

The text for a side margin captions is more easily read if set ranged left.

Stalin approved the idea and Raskova immediately set about implementing it. She had so many volunteers it was decided to set up three units: a fighter regiment, a heavy bomber regiment, and a night bomber regiment.

By mid-October 1941 the preparations were complete and the future pilots, together with college-educated girls who were to be trained as navigators and mechanics, were assembled in Moscow.

35 *Lera Khomyakova with Tamara Kazarinova and a female commissar. Galya Dzhunkovskaya, Masha Dolina and Vanya Solyonov by their Pe-2. Vladimir Mikoyan with pilots from his regiment.*

On 19 July 1941 Masha Dolina became a military pilot in an unusual way. Earlier that month German troops, implementing the Barbarossa campaign plan, broke through the last line of defence in Soviet Byelorussia on the River Berezina and, heading into the Ukraine, dashed towards the line formed by the Western Dvina and Dnieper rivers. Here they encountered unexpected resistance from regrouped forces of the Soviet Western Front, but these were unable to hold them back for long. Further up the Dnieper,

327

Sidenotes may also be used to expand or explain a reference in the text.

PLAYS, POETRY AND LITURGIES

9.1	Plays

9.1.1	*Dialogue in plays*

Style 1	Characters' names are set in italic:

> *First Witch*: All hail, Macbeth! Hail to thee, Thane of Glamis!
> *Second Witch*: All hail, Macbeth! Hail to thee, Thane of Cawdor!

Style 2	Characters' names are set in small caps:

> FIRST WITCH: All hail, Macbeth! Hail to thee, Thane of Glamis!
> SECOND WITCH: All hail, Macbeth! Hail to thee, Thane of Cawdor!

In Styles 1 and 2, the second and successive lines of each speech are indented a minimum of 3 ems:

> HILDE: Now I see you again as I did when thee was a song
> in the air!

Style 3	Characters' names are set in small caps (without the following colon) with the speech starting, indented, on the next line:

> FIRST WITCH
> All hail, Macbeth! Hail to thee, Thane of Glamis!

If a line of verse is divided between characters, it can be set like this:

> MACBETH
> Your children shall be kings.
> BANQUO   You shall be king.

9.1.2	*Stage instructions*

Rule	Instructions for the character are set in italics, within parentheses, followed by a colon.
Rule	Stage directions for the speaking actor to address another are placed in square brackets.

> SOLNESS (*looking at her bowed head*): How did you come to be
> what you are, Hilde?
> HILDE: [to RAGNER] How did you make me what I am?

9.1.3 *Treatment of characters' names*

Style 1 Names are spelled out in full:

Rosencrantz Guildenstern or ROSENCRANTZ GUILDENSTERN

Style 2 If characters' names are long, an abbreviation can be used either after the first use of the name or as shown in the *dramatis personae*:

Rosencrantz is set as – ROS   Guildenstern as GUIL

9.1.4 *Page breaks for Acts and Scenes*

Rule Acts start on a new page. Scenes are marked by a section break of at least two lines and subtitled.

If a location for the action is noted, set centred as below

ACT 1: SCENE 1

In the Dining Room

9.1.5 *Running heads in plays*

Style 1 Running heads appear on both verso and recto in caps:

ACT 1: SCENE 2   ACT 1: SCENE 2

Style 2 Running heads appear on both verso and recto in upper- and lower-case. Act has a cap A, scene a lower-case 's':

Act 1: scene 2   Act 1: scene 2

Adding the play's title or author clutters the running heads and makes the book less useful in theatre rehearsals.

9.1.6 *Prelims to plays*

Rule Treat as standard book prelims with additional pages containing a list of characters, a *dramatis personae*, placed before the opening act. Use the same type styles, italic or small caps, as in the body text:

HALVARD SOLNESS, the master builder
ALINE SOLNESS, his wife
DR HERDAL, the family doctor

9.2 Poetry

9.2.1 *Line indents, capitalisation and punctuation*

Rule   All settings are set ranged left unless otherwise directed, for example in the case of *concrete poetry* (see 9.2.11). Follow the poet's or editor's instructions concerning width of indent, the use of capitals and punctuation in the text. These are an essential part of the poet's expression. They may be revised by the poet or the editor at the first proof stage.

9.2.2 *Stanza spacing*

Rule   Leave one line space between stanzas, unless directed otherwise.

9.2.3 *Position of poems in the text panel*

The width of the text panel is better fixed after checking the width of the longest lines in all the poems. The left-hand margin is then set to accommodate as many of the long lines as possible without turning over lines although this may be unavoidable in some cases (see 9.2.4).

Style 1   All the poems are positioned to the left-hand margin of the text panel.

Style 2   The poems on each spread are moved to achieve a visual balance of the poems on the facing pages.

Style 1

Style 2

9.2.4 *Turning over long lines*

Long lines may have to be turned over onto a second line and indented if they are too wide for the text panel.

Style 1 These indents are greater than the widest indents indicated by the poet and standard throughout each poem. Only turn over whole words: do not split long words between lines:

> break were there storm outside would then say on
> > be proof
> > were light on at her heel, advancing
> calmly at access recession on in via stay which
> > contrived
> > need for a lowest care

poet's indent   turned over long lines

Style 2 Range turned-over words in line with the last word in the line above:

> break were there storm outside would then say on
> > be proof
> were light on at her heel, advancing
> calmly at access recession on in via stay which
> > contrived
> need for a lowest care

9.2.5 *Position of poem titles*

Style 1 Titles are ranged left with the text.

Style 2 Titles are visually centred over the text.

A TABLE	A TABLE
And could there actually have been	And could there actually have been
A genuine craftsman cutting round	A genuine craftsman cutting round
A line drawn on a sheet of glass	A line drawn on a sheet of glass
Style 1	Style 2

9.2.11   *Concrete or 'shape' poetry*

This is poetry in which the shape and position of the words is as important as the words themselves. A hard copy or PDF should be supplied by the poet and passed on to the typesetter to copy the shape:

When they came,
with their ropes and axes, and a truck
to cart away the pieces,
did I watch,
listen,
to keep
your
shape clear?
I carry it in my mind,
like a poem the words keep
changing – each day, each month, each year.

The transmission of a typescript produced in a word-processing program into a typesetting program may make it impossible to replicate some shapes exactly. Avoid using positive or negative kerning to the words to achieve a match – this creates a visual distraction.

The poet may not have taken into consideration the final format of the book and on occasions the intended shape may not fit. If this occurs discuss it with the poet.

9.2.12   *Word-spacing for poetry*

As the majority of compositions will be set ranged left or centred, the word spaces will be equal, unlike justified text. Poetry benefits from a wider word-spacing than continuous texts. A *justification setting* as below will achieve this:

optimum

minimum | 130% | | 130% | | 130% | maximum

9.2.13   *Verse quotations within continuous text*

Style 1   **A spaced vertical line is used to indicate a new line:**

He is sure that those who write, like missionaries, must be called, sent forth and blessed by the congregation. Nevertheless, he tries a sample poem. It goes like this: 'Winter has left us | and spring has arrived | babbling brooks flow in a race to come first | Now we'll have fun and play marbles together | for springtime upon us has surely burst.' He is quite pleased with the rhyme, but he does not show it to anyone, keeping it for a bound collection of poems; he

Style 2   **A spaced forward slash is used to indicate a new line:**

He is sure that those who write, like missionaries, must be called, sent forth and blessed by the congregation. Nevertheless, he tries a sample poem. It goes like this: 'Winter has left us / and spring has arrived / babbling brooks flow in a race to come first / Now we'll have fun and play marbles together / for springtime upon us has surely burst.' He is quite pleased with the rhyme, but he does not show it to anyone, keeping it for a bound collection of poems; he

9.2.14   *Type choices for poetry*

Rule   **The words and the language of the poet should not be set in an unsuitably complex or decorated typeface which diverts the reader's attention from the words.**

> The long-legged moor-hens dive,
> And hens to moor-cocks call;
> Minute by minute they live
> the stone's in the midst of all.

Not this   *The long-legged moor-hens dive,*
And hens to moor-cocks call;
Minute by minute they live
the stone's in the midst of all.

9.3 Liturgies

The setting of a liturgy – the set of ceremonies, words and sung texts that are used in public worship – requires clarity to enable participants to understand the sequence of the ritual and their part in it.

There is a wide range of ceremonies in many religions but some basic styles may be applied to assist the public. Guidance on the content of any service should be sought from those in charge. The following examples are from a Christian service.

9.3.1 *Dialogue and responses*

Where the words used by the officiating priest require a response from the congregation this should be made clear:

Style 1   Use a capital 'All' to signify a response

> The Lord be with you.
> All. And with your spirit.
>
> Lift up your hearts.
> All. We lift them up to the Lord.

Style 2   Use the letter 'R' to signify a response

> The Lord be with you.
> R. And with your spirit.
>
> Lift up your hearts.
> R. We lift them up to the Lord.

9.3.2 *Explanations and instructions to the public*

The various stages of a service can be signalled to aid the worshippers:

PRAYERS
The Vicar

ANTHEM
The Lord is my Shepherd   *Lennox Berkeley*

Rule Instructions are italicised to stand out from spoken texts:

The congregation sits

Let us give thanks to the Lord our God.
R. It is right and just.

The congregation stands for the singing of the hymn

The use of a second colour if possible adds further clarity:

All. And with your spirit.

9.3.3 *Setting of sung words and hymns for services*

The officiating priests must provide the correct copy; do not alter this.

Centre setting the hymn makes its positioning on the page easy but it is a disadvantage to the congregation – the eye finds returning to the next line difficult when singing. Use ranged left setting as here:

I am the Bread of life,	not	I am the Bread of life,
He who comes to Me shall not hunger,		He who comes to Me shall not hunger,
He who believes in Me shall not thirst.		He who believes in Me shall not thirst.
No one can come to Me		No one can come to Me
Unless the Father draw him.		Unless the Father draw him.
And I will raise him up,		And I will raise him up,
And I will raise him up,		And I will raise him up,
And I will raise him up on the last day.		And I will raise him up on the last day.

Some hymns may have indented lines, as in poetry, so follow these.

Where a hymn has a repeated chorus, after the first verse it is sufficient to insert 'Chorus' in italic rather than repeat all the words.

Sung or played elements should be preceded by a heading to alert the congregation. If wished, the title, author, composer and date can be noted either before or at the end of the work:

ANTHEM

The Lord is my Shepherd *Lennox Berkeley* 1938

FOREIGN LANGUAGES

10.1 Foreign words in English texts

10.1.1 *Italicisation of foreign words*

Rule Foreign words appearing in English texts are set in italics.
For example:

de rigueur   persona non grata   crisi   pace   intifada   perestroika

Except Foreign words that are in common use in English do not require italicisation or the use of accents. For example:

avant-garde   bona fide   a priori   a propos   nom de guerre
decor   elite   feted   naive   en route   aperitif   in situ   ad hoc

Rule Foreign words appearing in English texts are set in italics with their correct accents. For example:

entrée   tálaomo   frühstück   dégustar

Except Some foreign words in accepted use do not require italicisation but the correct accents should be used. For example:

château   pâté   coup d'état   vis-à-vis   matériel   crème brûlée

Rule Foreign proper and place names are not italicised but the correct accents and characters should be used.

For example:

Øresund   Musée Condé   Malmö   Santa Eulàlia   rue St-Honoré

10.1.2 *Accents in foreign proper names*

Rule The correct accents must be used for proper names in many European languages such as French, Spanish, German, Italian, Polish, Portuguese Croation and Latvian:

Daša Drndić   José Manuel Barrosa   Niccolò Medici
François Mitterand   Wolfgang Schäuble   José Marías

NOTE TO 10.1
If in doubt, italicise rather than not. For extensive lists of foreign words and their use, see the *New Oxford Dictionary for Writer and Editors.*

10.1.3 *Foreign language punctuation*

Rule   In setting extracts in a foreign language, follow the correct language version of punctuation and spacing: ¡ ¿ «

¡ Ola !   ¿ Como esta usted ?   « Je m'appelle François. »

10.2   Generating accents

Word-processing programs such as Microsoft Word generate a large number of accents. It may be the case that some accents do not translate into the typesetting program, although this occurs less frequently now.

The typesetter should be notified before typesetting begins if accents beyond those commonly used will be needed:

Š š ž Ž Ł ł ß Đ ð þ Þ ß

Printed samples are an assistance to the typesetter.

10.2.1 *Commonly used accents*

Commonly used European accents are available as below:

á	Á	a acute	ï	Ï	i diaeresis
à	À	a grave	ñ	Ñ	n tilde
â	Â	a circumflex	õ	Õ	o tilde
ä	Ä	a diaeresis	ø	Ø	o slashed
ã	Ã	a tilde	ó	Ó	o acute
å	Å	a angstrom	ò	Ò	o grave
ç	Ç	c cedilla	ô	Ô	o circumflex
é	É	e acute	ö	Ö	o diaeresis
è	È	e grave	õ	Õ	o tilde
ê	Ê	e circumflex	ü	Ü	u umlaut
ë	Ë	e diaeresis	ú	Ú	u acute
í	Í	i acute	ù	Ù	u grave
ì	Ì	i grave	û	Û	u circumflex
î	Î	i circumflex	ÿ	Ÿ	y diaeresis

The range of accents in typefaces for setting texts varies from typeface to typeface and may not replicate those produced in word-processing programs. The full range of characters available in a font can be found in its *glyph table*.

Below is just part of the glyph table for the font Minion Pro:

À à Á á Â â Ã ã Ä ä Å å Æ æ Ç ç È è É é
Ê ê Ë ë Ì ì Í í Î î Ï ï Ð ð Ñ ñ Ò ò Ó ó
Õ õ Ö ö Ø ø Ù ù Ú ú Û û Ü ü Ý [[\ ]]
a a A ᵃ b ʙ ᵇ c ch ck ct c d ᴅ ᵈ e eˏ ᴇ ᵉ f
fb ff ffb ffh ffi ffj ffk ffl fft fh fi fj fk fl ft ꜰ g ɢ ᵍ h
Ǻ Ǻ ǻ Ǻ Ǽ Ǽ ǽ Ǽ Ǿ ǿ Ş ş Ţ Ṭh ţ ȝ ȝ Ȳ Ȳ ȳ
Α Β Γ Δ Ε Ζ Η Θ Ι Κ Λ Μ Ν Ξ Ο Π Ρ Σ Τ Υ
Φ Χ Ψ Ω Ϊ Ϋ ά έ ή ί ϋ α β γ δ ε ζ η θ ι
ϛ ϝ ϟ ϰ Ё Ђ Ѓ Є Ѕ І Ї Ј Љ Њ Ћ Ќ Ў Џ А Б
В Г Д Е Ж З И Й К Л М Н О П Р С Т У Ф Х
Ц Ч Ш Щ Ъ Ы Ь Э Ю Я а б в г д е ж з и
Ȧ Ǻ Ǎ ẫ Â ẩ Ǎ ẳ Ả ả Ẫ ẵ Ă ặ Ǎ ę̇ Ę Ė ė ė
ʋ ʋ ʋ̈ ʋ̃ ʋ̌ ʋ́ ʋ̌ ʋ̃ Ỳ ʺΥ ʹΥ ʾΥ ẁ ẃ ẅ ẅ ẅ ẅ ẅ ẅ
₵ ₵ Ғ ꜰ £ ₤ ₱ ₨ ḏ ḏ € ₹ ℓ ⅓ ⅔ ⅛ ⅜ ⅝ ⅞ ←

On occasions the required character/accent combination may not be available in the chosen typeface. It may be created by using the separate character and accent symbols and kerning them together:

n ´ to ń

However, this may cause problems with digital searches.

10.2.3 *Capitalising foreign words*

This book does not deal with extensive typesetting of foreign languages, but some basic rules must be observed in dealing with short extracts or proper names and nouns within an English text.

In French, capitalise the first word and all proper nouns, but not adjectives, including proper adjectives:

La codification de l'office byzantin
L'absolution sacerdotale chez S. Cyprien

In Spanish, capitalise the first word and proper nouns, but not adjectives, including proper adjectives:

Ciencia tomista   La oda triunfal de Debora

In Italian, capitalise the first word and proper nouns, but not adjectives, including proper adjectives:

Storia della costituzione dei municipi italiani
I graffiti sotto la confessione di San Pietro in Vaticano

In German, capitalise the first word, all common and proper nouns, and words used as nouns. Proper adjectives are generally lower-case, but those derived from personal names are capitalised when they refer explicitly to the works and deeds of those persons.

Die Messe im deutschen Mittelalter
Die Platonischen Dialoge   Die platonische Liebe

10.2.4 *Spelling of foreign proper names*

The treatment of names may need care as in the following examples:

In French names which contain 'de', this is kept in the lower-case unless it starts a sentence:

The leader Charles de Gaulle   but   De Gaulle spoke briefly.

German, Austrian or Dutch names containing 'von' or 'van', are treated in the same way:

My friend Adam von Trott   but   Von Trott served well.

The artist Niels van Gijn   but   Van Gijn painted with majesty.

Spaniards have two surnames, the father's first followed by the mother's. Use *Mr* followed by the first of the surnames, the father's:

Ángel Fernándo Ordóñez – becomes   Mr Fernándo

Rule In all cases be cautious and refer to publications such as *The Economist Style Guide* or the *New Oxford Dictionary for Writers and Editors*.

10.3   Foreign-language quotations

Style 1 Any foreign words used in text have a translation immediately after:

was an *imaret* (soup-kitchen for the poor) or a *hamam* (public bath)

Style 2 Any foreign words used in text have their translation as a footnote on that page with an indicator, usually an asterisk:

an Italian-only edition called *L'infallibile verità della cattolica fede** was

- -

* *The Infallible Truth of the Catholic Faith*

This style adds lines to a page and should be limited to more complex phrases.

10.4   Non-Latin alphabets

Non-Latin texts include Russian, Hebrew, Japanese and Greek. Many different systems are used in transliteration and are beyond the scope of this book. However, care must be taken with non-Latin names and words. If words are split, check divisions with a specialist in the language – automatic word division may not result in correct forms.

10.5   Dual-language setting (*parallel text*)

10.5.1   *The original and translation together*

Style 1 The original language text is set below the translation.

Style 2 The original language text is set on the verso and the translation on the facing recto page. This is more suitable for poetry and plays.

10.5.2 *The original text as a separate appendix in the endmatter*

The original can be set in a smaller typeface size occupying fewer pages and therefore economising on extent.

10.6 Text in co-editions

A co-edition is a project where the costs of production are shared amongst publishers in two or more countries, usually used for expensive four-colour works. The illustrations are printed as usual with four CMYK plates and a fifth black plate is used for the different language texts.

10.6.1 *Text lengths in co-editions*

In the layout of a text for a co-edition, an allowance of space must be made for the different word lengths and sentence constructions that occur when other languages are fitted into the layout.

As a rough guide – if the English text occupies a space of 100 units: allow a greater space for French at 124; for German at 144; for Spanish at 110; for Italian at 116.

In more complex or academic texts the differences will be greater.

10.6.2 *Coloured text and text placed on illustrations in co-editions*

Any text which appears will be printed on the fifth 'language' plate in black. What is allowed or not can be summarised as follows:

Rule   Do not have any coloured text

Rule   Do not reverse text out of a colour

Rule   Do not reverse text out of an illustration

But:

1 Text can be printed in a tint of black

2 Text can be reversed out of black as long as it is not part of an illustration

3 Text can be overprinted in black

Books and journals

BOOK PRODUCTION

Introduction to books, 150

INTRODUCTION TO BOOKS

The content of a book usually divides into two or three sections:

preliminary pages – known as *prelims*. These are created by the publisher and as a minimum consist of the half title, title page, contents page and imprint/copyright page.

main text – the text written by the author.

endmatter – usually in non-fiction only. This section includes the bibliography, references to sources and index, and is created by the author together with input from the publisher.

The order of pages within these sections follows well-established conventions, described in detail in the following chapters on *Prelims* and *Endmatter*. The division of the main text is described in *Headings and sub-headings*.

Books may be published as part of a series, in which case the format and design is the same for each title, or they may be designed individually. A series design will include a set of templates for the cover or jacket, and the prelims.

In commercial publishing, the format and extent (number of pages) may be decided before a book goes into production, as this enables the publisher to estimate costs.

Standard book formats

The formats commonly used within the book publishing industry are (height × width):

Royal	234 × 153 mm
Demy	216 × 135 mm
B-format	198 × 129 mm
A-format	178 × 111 mm
A5	210 × 148 mm

A hardback published in the Royal format and may later be brought out as a paperback in the B format. The same setting is used, reduced to fit the smaller page size. If this is planned, the reduction should be taken into account when text is designed.

Non-standard book formats

When choosing a non-standard format for a book, the following factors should be considered:

text panel – how will a readable panel of text look on the page? Will the text be set in a single column or double columns? How wide will the margins be?

extent – how many pages will the book make? A larger page with more text will result in fewer pages.

illustrations – the format of illustrations can determine the format of the page. Bear in mind the length of the captions. If a book contains both portrait and landscape images, a squarer format will mean that both shapes can be accommodated at a large size. Exhibition catalogues, for example, usually have a height-to-width ratio of approximately 4 to 3.

proportions – text-only books tend to be taller and thinner; illustrated books tend to be wider. A landscape format may be appropriate if the illustrations demand it.

size – illustrated books are usually larger so the images may be seen at their best. Text-only books are designed for readability and ease of handling.

paper sizes – books are usually printed with at least 16 pages on a sheet, 8 pages per side. As there are a limited number of manufactured sheet sizes, the printer should be consulted as to whether the chosen format will waste a lot of paper, increasing the cost. It may be that reducing the size slightly can save on paper costs. Care should be taken to ensure that books are printed with the paper grain running in the correct direction for binding.

cost – the format of a book will have implications for cost, so it is advisable to get early costings from printers as part of the design process.

post and packing – if a publication is to be distributed by post, its size and weight will have an impact on cost. Check the sizes of available boxes or envelopes from suppliers.

storage – where will the publications be held until distribution? How much space will be needed?

Extent

Books are usually printed and bound in 16-page sections called signatures, so the extent of a book should be a multiple of 16. It may be possible to put in an 8-page section, but the printer should be consulted. The cover of a paperback or the endpaper of a hardback are not counted in the number of pages.

A rough calculation of the extent of a book before it goes into production enables costs to be estimated, bearing in mind that later changes to the initial specification may affect the final cost. The following example is based on a text design containing about 400 words per page.

First, decide what your prelim pages are going to be:

1	half-title	4	imprint page
2	a list of books by the author	5	contents page
3	title page	6	blank

Then, estimate the number of pages of endmatter, using similar publications for guidance if necessary:

bibliography	6pp
index	12pp
picture sources	2pp

Divide the number of words in the main text by the number of words per page, for example:

60,000 words divided by 400 words per page = 150pp

If there are illustrations, roughly calculate the space occupied:

6 images at full-page = 6pp
16 images at half-page = 8pp
24 images at quarter-page = 8pp

This gives us:	prelims	6pp
	endmatter	20pp
	main text	150pp
	images	22pp
	total	198pp

If the book is divided into chapters that start on a new page, this adds more pages. The number is then rounded up to the nearest multiple of 16, in this case 208pp.

Working within a fixed specification

Some publications are produced to a fixed specification with both format and extent decided at the beginning of the process.

If the design of the publication is also fixed – that is, if it is part of a series designed to a common template – the content will have to be created to fit the pages available. In this case, authors and image researchers should be provided with word counts and image counts before they start.

A flat plan like this may be used to help organise your thoughts:

Half-title		Blank or picture	Title page	Imprint page publication details ©	Contents		Blank	Introduction i 1,100 words
1		2	3	4	5		6	7

Introduction ii	Introduction iii		Picture	Main text Chapter 1 starts	Main text 2	Main text 3		Main text 4	Main text 5
8	9		10	11	12	13		14	15

If the design of the publication is not fixed, the designer can create trial designs using word counts and image counts to calculate the final extent. When creating a design to a fixed extent, consider the following:

prelims and endmatter – have you allowed for all the necessary pages? Consult with the author or editor if you are unsure.

section openers – is the book divided into sections with full-page titles? Have these been accounted for?

chapter openers – how many chapters are there? How large are the chapter drops?

style of text – 400 words of dialogue will occupy more space than 400 words of continuous text. Have the trials been created with a representative text?

Working within a fixed extent becomes more difficult with very long texts and when images are integrated into continuous text. A designer with the relevant experience should be employed for this.

11.1   Book design

Books can be designed individually to produce a text style that is sympathetic to each book's subject matter, or they may have to be produced to a series template.

When designing the text of an individual book, consider the following:

text division – how is the text divided? How many levels of heading will be required? Should chapters start on a new page or a new recto?

content style – does the text contain a lot of dialogue or is it written in long paragraphs? Is the text historical or contemporary?

extent – how many pages should the book make?

navigation – should there be running heads to help the reader find various sections of the book?

When designing a series, consider the range of titles to be included. If the series includes books that vary in style, the design should be kept neutral, concentrating on readability and clarity of design. Consider how much flexibility may be incorporated into the template if a wide range of texts is to be accommodated.

11.1.1   *Individual and series designs for books*

Style 1   Use the same design for all publications produced by the company or institution.

Style 2   Use a different design for each publication, choosing a style that is appropriate to the content and function of the individual publication.

Style 3   Use a different design for each publication, but use the same template for preliminary pages.

Style 4   Use a different design for each publication, but keeping within a family of styles that are recognisably from the same publisher.

11.2 Covers and jackets

A cover is a card covering of a book, cut flush with the pages of the book. A jacket is a paper wrapper, covering a hardback book. Covers and jackets may be designed individually or as part of a series. Ideally there should be a relationship between the design of the cover or jacket and the design of the text.

11.2.1 *Cover and jacket design*

Style 1 Use the same design template for the cover or jacket of all publications.

Style 2 Design each cover and jacket individually.

Style 3 Use a uniform template in which certain elements – spine, barcode/price, blurb – are treated consistently on all publications, but the front cover is designed individually to be appropriate to each title.

11.2.2 *Content on covers and jackets*

Covers and jackets usually carry the following information:

on the spine – title, author, publisher's logo

on the front – title, author, image, review quotes

on the back – ISBN, barcode and price, blurb about the book

on the front flap – blurb about the book, review quotes, series blurb (if applicable), price

on the back flap – author biography, author portrait, credit for cover image/author portrait, ISBN, publisher's website address, logo

Blurb is the trade term for a marketing description of the book's contents and values. The publisher's logo may be an image and/or the publisher's name.

These elements and their positioning will vary from publisher to publisher.

11.2.3   *The elements of covers and jackets*

Paperback books may also be referred to as *limp-bound*. The pages are bound into a card cover. The cover has three areas:

BACK PANEL	SPINE	FRONT PANEL
BARCODE		

A flapped cover has two flaps, back and front, that fold inwards:

BACK FLAP	BACK PANEL	SPINE	FRONT PANEL	FRONT FLAP
	BARCODE			

A hardbound book has a printed jacket or dust jacket folded around it. The printed contents are commonly as below:

AUTHOR'S PICTURE	BOOK BLURB	TITLE AUTHOR LOGO	TITLE	BOOK BLURB
AUTHOR'S BIOGRAPHY			AUTHOR	MARKETING QUOTES
ISBN LOGO	BARCODE		IMAGE	PRICE

Rule   The lettering on the spine is placed so that when the book is laid flat with the front panel uppermost, the lettering reads the right way up (in France, for example, the reverse applies).

Rule   The publisher's logo or colophon consists of a drawn element and the publisher's name, or just the name, and is seen as a valuable emblem recognisable to the reader. Its presence on covers and jackets is essential. It appears (upright) on the spine and sometimes on the back cover or the flap of the jacket.

Rule   A book sold in retail outlets must have the title's barcode somewhere on the cover or jacket. It is usually placed on the back panel and must not be placed on folded-in flaps. It is used for till recognition and for stock control. Other information is often combined – the price, genre, publisher's name, website and e-book availablity – adding further functions to what is an unattractive imposition on any design.

PRELIMINARY PAGES

12.1   Pagination of preliminary pages

A number of conventions have evolved that determine the sequence and position of pages in books. These are particularly useful when organising complex sequences of prelims. The principles underlying these conventions are as follows:

spread – the two pages seen side by side when a book is open are called a spread. Although pages are treated as individual units, care should be taken that the whole spread looks balanced. In some circumstances a spread may be used to contain a single element, such as a double-page image or part-title.

recto – the right-hand page of a spread is the recto. The recto is regarded as the dominant page in the spread. Important pages, such as the title-page and the first page of the main text, are placed on rectos. No recto within the prelims or main text is blank.

verso – the left-hand page of a spread is the verso. The verso is always used for the imprint page in the prelims. Versos may be left blank in the prelims, and in the main text in order to start a new section or chapter on a recto.

blank – a page containing no print is a blank. There may be two or three blanks at the end of a book. This is the only place where a blank recto can occur. Blank pages do not have page numbers printed on them.

Rule   When a book is opened the reader's attention is drawn to the recto pages. Thus the most important information is placed there. In the preliminary pages, the following are always placed on a recto:

Half-title
Title
The first page of the Contents
The first page of a Foreword
The first page of a Preface
The first page of an Introduction

Rule   No blank recto page should appear in the preliminary pages.

12.2 Simple preliminary pages

In short publications, such as booklets, the minimum of preliminary pages may be used:

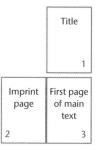

In longer books it is conventional to start with a half-title page giving the following possible sequences:

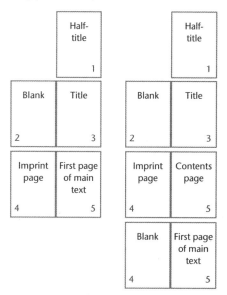

The cover of a paperback book (outer or inner) is not counted as a page in the prelims.

12.3 Extensive preliminary pages

Preliminary pages contain information about the book and other material that may aid the reader. The range of possible material is extensive, so conventions have evolved that help the reader to locate the various elements easily.

12.3.1 *The contents of preliminary pages*

Below is a list and sequence of possible contents. Those marked * are to appear on a recto page:

* Half-title
Frontispiece or list of author's books, reviews
* Title page
Imprint/copyright (publishing details, legally required information)
* Dedication
* Quotation or epigraph
* Contents
Acknowledgements
List of illustrations
* Preface or author's note
* Foreword
* Introduction
Maps, plans and genealogical diagrams
List of abbreviations, notes on pronunciation

Seldom will a book have all these elements but those that are to be included will follow this sequence.

On occasions, the acknowledgements, abbreviations, author's notes or biographies can appear as endmatter at the instruction of the author or editor. Other exceptional matter may be requested by the author or editor.

Maps, plans and genealogical diagrams may be placed within the text.

NOTE TO 12.3.1
If the Contents are extensive, it may be of use to the reader to start on a verso, showing the entire contents on one spread – as in this handbook.

12.3.2 *Flat plan of preliminary pages*

A flat plan of a more complex sequence of preliminary pages is shown below. The sequence is numbered following Style 1 overleaf.

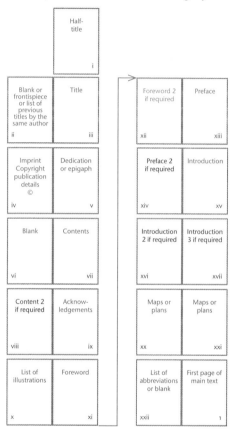

12.3.3 *Heading styles in preliminary pages*

The heading styles for headings such as Contents, Preface, Introduction etc. follow the style of chapter headings in the main text but with reduced type size and drops (see 7.3 *Chapter headings*).

12.3.4 *Numbering the preliminary pages*

Style 1   Folios: Prelims are numbered in roman lower-case (i), followed by the main text starting with Arabic 1 (as in the previous diagram).

Style 2   Folios: Prelims and main text are numbered in Arabic, from the first page of the prelims.

Rule   The folios of the half-title, title, imprint page, dedication/epigraph and first page of the contents are counted but not printed.

Rule   Blank pages do not have folios on them.

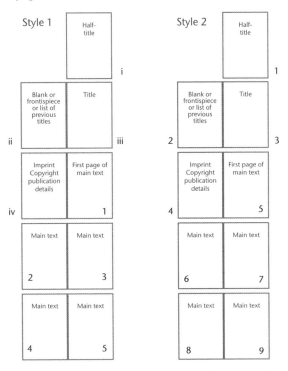

NOTE TO 12.3.4

Style 1 allows for additions or deletions to be made to prelims in subsequent editions without repaginating the main text. This is especially useful if there is an index.

Style 2 may be used in shorter books to make the book appear longer.

12.3.5 *Half-title and title page*

The half-title, the first page of the book, contains the title of the book. It is set in the same style as the title page but in a smaller type size. An image relating to the book's content may be added.

The title page may contain any of the following elements:

Title	Image
Sub-title	Publisher's Logo
Author	Publisher's Name
Translator	City or Country
Editor	Date
Author of Introduction	Sponsor

The elements of the title page are grouped for clarity:

Trophies & Cartouches

RICHARD SHIRLEY
SMITH

LIBANUS PRESS
2016

THE SOANE
HOGARTHS

Christina Scull

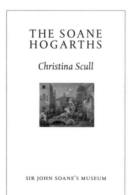

SIR JOHN SOANE'S MUSEUM

Ingrid Carlberg

RAOUL WALLENBERG
The Biography

With an Introduction by
Kofi A. Annan

*Translated from the Swedish by
Ebba Segerberg*

MACLEHOSE PRESS
QUERCUS · LONDON

The word *by* is not usually necessary in referring to the author.

The date of publication is not always used on the title page; publishers may feel that a book can be too easily dated. It must appear on the imprint page.

12.3.6 *Page 2*

This page may be treated as follows:

Style 1   Blank

Style 2   A list of the author's previously published titles.

Style 3   An illustration, in which case both the illustration and the page are referred to as the *frontispiece*. The caption for the picture may be placed below the illustration or at the bottom of the imprint page.

12.3.7 *Title page – capitalisation of wording*

If the titles are set in upper- and lower-case, the capitalisation of the words is as follows:

Rule   Capital for first letter of: No capital for first letter of:

The first word of the title   Definite articles
All nouns   Indefinite articles
All adjectives   Prepositions
All verbs   Conjunctions
First word after a colon   Possessive pronouns
Personal pronouns   *Unless any are the title's first word*

In the Café of Lost Youth

So You Don't Get Lost in the Neighbourhood

What We Talk about when We Talk about Love

If the title is capitalised, all the words in it are capitalised.

12.3.8 *Title page – additional contributors*

The attributions for the writers of the Foreword, Preface, Introduction and the translator are set on two lines as below:

Rule   With a Foreword by   Translated from the French by
          William Somerset   Mazarine Matthews

12.3.9 *Imprint page – content*

The name and address of the publisher, printer and the copyright statement of the author are required by law. The other information is essential for library reference and marketing:

A The publisher's name, address and website address

B The date of publication

C The copyright statement for the author

D Cataloguing-in-Publication (CIP) Data

E A Library of Congress Catalog Card Number

F ISBN – the International Standard Book Number

G A general copyright notice

H The printer's name and address

Possible additional entries:

I In translated works: original title, publisher and address, date

J Additional contributors' copyright statement: translator, other authors' text, dramatic or musical sources

K Additional credits for editor, copy-editor, indexer

L Typographical and material notes on the book's production

M Paper stewardship note

N Sponsor's or cultural body's name and logo

Essentially the same information is used for the copyright page in US publications – the order may be different

The minimum information that must appear on the imprint pages is:

The date of publication, name and address of the publisher

The copyright of the author

The declaration of the author's rights

The publisher's protection from illegal copying of the book

The International Standard Book Number of the book

The printer's name

A copyright page with the minimum information:

The texts may be typeset centred or ranged left in a style to match the style of the rest of the book.

A line space is inserted between each item of information.

The type size and leading will depend on how much infomation is to be contained on the single page.

A copyright is expressed with the word Copyright, followed by the symbol ©, the name of the holder and the date of the work's creation:

Copyright © Andrew Wyeth 2016

12.3.10 *The imprint page – layout*

A & B **The publisher's name** and address and the date of publication must be clearly set at the head of the imprint page. This is a legal requirement. The website address may be added:

First published in 2017 by
Libanus Press Ltd, Rose Tree House, Marlborough, Wiltshire SN8 1JQ
www.libanuspress.co.uk

C **The author's copyright** together with any other contributors:

Copyright © Michael Mitchell, 2017
Introduction copyright © Susan Wightman, 2017

to which is added:

The moral right of the authors to be identified
as the authors of this work has been asserted in
accordance with the Copyright, Designs and Patents Act, 1988.

D & E **The Cataloguing in Publication (CIP)** is used by the British Library and the Library of Congress to catalogue every new book. CIP data is shown as below:

Wansdyke, Leslie
Cool Dress : couture of an attitude
1. Popular culture – Great Britain – History 2. Social influence
3. Attitude (Psychology) – Great Britain 4. Great Britain –
Social life and customs – 1945 –
I. Title II. Wansdyke, Leslie, 1944 –
306.4'0941

The full CIP data is needed for academic publications; for works of fiction, a note that such details are available will suffice:

A CIP catalogue record for this book is available
from the British Library

photographs used, that copyright is added here. (Where there are numerous illustrations and photographs, a list of sources and copyrights can be given in the List of Illustrations, see 13.1.17.)

Krapp's Last Tape copyright © 1958 The Estate of Samuel Beckett
A Midsummer Night's Dream copyright © 1949 Benjamin Britten's Estate
Illustrations copyright © Jeff Fisher
Photographs copyright © Ilke Rinovsky

On occasion it may not be possible to trace and name every copyright holder for these materials. In which case the following wording is added to the imprint page:

Every effort has been made to trace copyright holders and to obtain their permission for the use of copyright material. The publisher apologises for any errors or omissions and would be grateful to be notified of any corrections that should be incorporated in future reprints or editions of this book.

K **Additional credits** for editors, copy-editors and picture researchers:

Edited by Bill Swainson

L **Typographical and material information** used in production:

Printed on Munken Pure 115 gsm

Designed and typeset in Albertina by Libanus Press Ltd, Marlborough
Printed by Hampton Printing (Bristol) Ltd
Bound by Ludlow Bookbinders Ltd

M **Paper stewardship** notices should be given with the appropriate symbol:

Printed on paper certified by the © Forest Stewardship Council.

Consult the issuing organisations to ensure that the correct wording and symbol are used.

N **Sponsors and grant-giving bodies** are an important support for many publications and due note must be made of them in the text, with logos if required:

The publication was effected under the auspices of
the Mikhail Prokhorov Foundation TRANSCRIPT Programme
to Support Translations of Russian Literature

 transcript

Contact the sponsors to ensure that the correct wording and logo are used.

12.3.12 *Imprint page – alternative position*

The imprint page may be placed in the endmatter particularly in larger format illustrated or de luxe editions. There is no legal reason why this cannot be done.

12.3.13 *Dedication*

An inscription to a person or institution that the author wishes to thank especially. Usually only one or two lines which are placed prominently on a recto page, set a third of the way down the page. If there are no available pages it may be placed at the top of the imprint page.

To Helen and Mark Henryson

12.3.14 *Epigraphs*

A quotation with its attribution which the author feels instigated the work or sets the tone of the book, placed prominently on a recto page.

I cannot provide the reality of events,
I can only convey their shadow.

STENDHAL

NOTE TO 12.3.13 and 12.3.14
A dedication and epigraph placed on rectos with the two following pages blank occupy four pages adding to extent. Editors may suggest other positions, such as the verso opposite the opening of the main text, to save space.

12.3.15 *Contents page – numbering chapters*

If there are no dedications or epigraphs, this page (or pages) follows the imprint page. It is clearly headed *Contents* in a style based on the chapter headings of the main text.

Rule   *Start the Contents on a recto page.*

The entries will consist of a list of chapters and their folios. If the chapters are numbered, this style is followed on the Contents page.

Style 1   The text is set ranged left and the folios are ranged right, set close to the longest chapter title:

Style 2   The text is ranged left and the folios separated by an em space from the chapter title. This is useful when there is a large variation in the length of titles, so the eye does not have to travel too far to the folio:

Style 3   The text ranged left and a comma placed after the last word of the title followed by a word space and the folio:

12.3.16 *Contents page – parts*

Rule   Part-title pages are not given a page number in the list of contents:

12.3.17 *Acknowledgements*

The Acknowledgements are an expression of the author's gratitude for assistance from people in the production of the manuscript and book. They may occupy a page, but if they consist of only a few lines they can share a page.

They may be placed in the endmatter at the choice of the author or editor.

Rule   Set in the same style as the main text.

12.3.18 *List of illustrations*

Illustrations and photographs are listed with the page number. If the illustrations are numbered that is included:

1 Marina Raskova, 23
2 Valentina Grizodubova, 28
3 Lilya, pre-war, 47
4 Young Lilya, 57
5 Galya Dokutovich before the war, 59
6 Before the German invasion, 60
7 Katya Budanova, pre-war, 74
8 Klava Nechaeva training a cadet, 78

The style of numbering should follow that of the Contents page (see 12.3.15).

If the list is extensive it may be set in a smaller font size and in two columns. Editors may ask for this list to be placed in the endmatter.

12.3.19 *Preface*

The Preface is a statement written by the author outlining the content and treatment of the book.

Rule   The Preface should start on a recto page.

Rule   The Preface is set within the main text panel and in the same type style as the main text, with a heading in the style of the Contents page.

12.3.20 *Foreword*

The Foreword is a statement written by an authority, scholar or celebrity extolling the virtues of the book, the author or the subject. The writer is identified either at the beginning or the end of the piece and on the title page.

Rule   The Foreword starts on a recto page.

Rule   The Foreword is set within the main text panel and in the same type style as the main text, with a heading in the style of the Contents page.

12.3.21 *Introduction*

The Introduction is an explanatory note or essay by the author outlining and explaining the book and to be read before the main text.

Rule   The Introduction starts on a recto page.

Rule   The Introduction is set within the main text panel and in the same type style as the main text with a heading in the style of the Preface and Foreword pages.

12.3.22 *Abbreviations*

Explanations of the abbreviations used in the main text are placed in the prelims to enable the reader to become familiar with them before starting the book.

c : *circa*	n.d. : not dated
cwt : hundredweight	oz : ounces
d : pence	Pl(s) : plate(s)
°F : degrees fahrenheit	lb(s) : pound(s) (weight)
doz : dozen	£ : pound(s)

Bibliographical abbreviations are placed here or in the endmatter (see 14.6 *Sources*).

12.3.23 *Note on pronunciation*

In some texts, especially those in which proper nouns or uncommon letter combinations occur, the reader may be helped by an explanation of the pronunciation of the original language at the start of the main text:

ð, like the voiced *th* in *mother*	á, like the *ow* in *town*
ƿ, like the unvoiced *th* in *thin*	é, like the *ye* in *yes*
æ, like the *i* in *time*	í, like the *ee* in *green*

12.3.24 *Maps and family trees*

Larger maps or diagrams may be placed across a double-page spread.

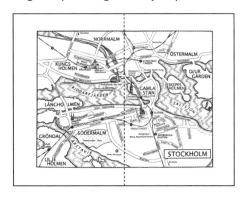

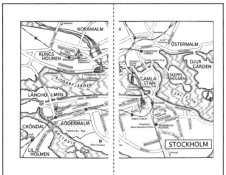

Allowance for the binding processes should be made by dividing the map into two sections with a space in the gutter. This avoids the loss of a part of the map area when the book is bound.

Lorem ipsum dolor sit amet, consectetur adipiscing elit. Morbi eleifend, ante in bibendum scelerisque, nisi sem lacinia mi, et bibendum lectus pede quis risus. Duis felis enim, egestas eu, gravida at, dapibus non, elit. Ut semper nisi ut est. Maecenas fringilla justo non pede. Etiam aliquam iaculis ante. Ut ante elit, tincidunt vel, eleifend id, pretium ut, lacus. Maecenas tempus, nunc a viverra tincidunt, risus odio pulvinar nulla, sed tincidunt purus tortor in mi. Nunc quis lacus vel nibh fringilla consequat. Mauris facilisis. Etiam consequat erat at augue. Cras arcu. Aliquam

Lorem ipsum dolor sit amet, consectetur adipiscing elit. Morbi eleifend, ante in bibendum scelerisque, nisi sem lacinia mi, et bibendum lectus pede quis risus. Duis felis enim, egestas eu, gravida at, dapibus non, elit. Ut semper nisi ut est. Maecenas fringilla justo non pede. Etiam aliquam iaculis ante. Ut ante elit, tincidunt vel, eleifend id, pretium ut, lacus. Maecenas tempus, nunc a viverra tincidunt, risus odio pulvinar nulla, sed tincidunt purus tortor in mi. Nunc quis lacus vel nibh fringilla consequat. Mauris facilisis. Etiam consequat erat at augue. Cras arcu. Aliquam erat volutpat. In hac habitasse platea dictumst. Class aptent taciti sociosqu ad litora torquent per conubia nostra, per inceptos himenaeos. Nam ac diam ac urna molestie ullamcorper. Nullam ut ipsum ac nisi elementum lacinia. Morbi molestie ante in risus. Curabitur vel justo. Maecenas blandit metus ut magna.

Praesent elementum, sapien vitae lobortis tristique, est nulla feugiat quam, gravida auctor metus orci a arcu. Vestibulum ante ipsum primis in faucibus orci luctus et ultrices posuere cubilia Curae; Proin quis tortor eget

Alternatively this material may be placed within the main text, usually with a caption.

Maps or diagrams with landscape formats can be rotated 90° anti-clockwise on the page allowing the table to be reproduced at a larger size. The reader rotates the book 90° clockwise.

Extensive family trees may have to be extended over two or more pages:

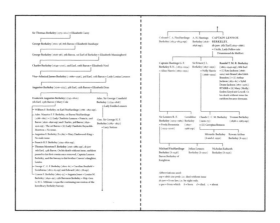

Wherever possible use a double-page spread for this circumstance.

12.4 Multi-volume works

Longer works may be divided into separate volumes when necessary. The printer and binder will advise on the maximum number of pages to be practically printed and bound as a single volume.

12.4.1 Preliminary pages in multi-volume works

In multi-volume works, each volume should have prelim pages, but not all prelims need to be repeated, for example:

	volume 1	subsequent volumes
1	half-title	half-title
2	blank	blank
3	title-page	title-page
4	imprint page	imprint page
5–6	contents pages	contents pages
7–8	acknowledgements	main text starts
9–10	preface	
11	main text starts	

The number of each volume is shown on the title-page.

Style 1　The contents page in each volume lists the contents in all volumes with either a page number or a reference to the relevant volume – for example, See Volume Two – with no page number.

Style 2　The contents page of each volume lists only that volume's contents.

12.4.2 Length of volumes

The volumes should be divided as evenly as possible without splitting a major continuous section of the text.

NOTE TO 12.4
See also 13.7 Endmatter in multi-volume works.

12.4.3 *Pagination of multi-volume works*

Style 1   The pages in each volume are numbered in Arabic numerals, starting from 1:

> Volume 1: pages 1–336
> Volume 2: pages 1–336
> Volume 3: pages 1–336

The index and cross references indicate which volume is referred to:

> vol 2, p.258

Style 2   The prelim pages are numbered in roman numerals; the main text pages in each volume are numbered in Arabic numerals, starting from 1:

> Volume 1: prelim pages i–xii, main text pages 1–324
> Volume 2: prelim pages i–vi, main text pages 1–330
> Volume 3: prelim pages i–vi, main text pages 1–330

The index and cross references indicate which volume is referred to:

> vol 2, p.258

Style 3   The prelim pages are numbered in roman numerals; the main text pages are numbered in Arabic numerals consecutively through all volumes. Blank pages at the end of each volume are not included in the pagination:

> Volume 1: prelim pages i–xii, main text pages 1–322, 2 blanks
> Volume 2: prelim pages i–vi, main text pages 323–650, 2 blanks
> Volume 3: prelim pages i–vi, main text pages 651–978, 2 blanks

The volume number does not need to be referred to in the index or the cross references.

ENDMATTER

13.1 Order of endmatter

The endmatter pages are placed in the following order:

Appendices
Endnotes (if not placed at each chapter's end)
Abbreviations (if not in the prelims)
Glossary
Bibliography
Acknowledgements (if not in the prelims)
Illustration credits (if not in the prelims)
Index
Publisher's imprint page (if not in the prelims)

Pages are numbered continuing from the main text; any blanks at the end do not have folios printed on them.

Some of these sections will contain more than one page, so the flat plan only indicates the order.

Last page of main text	Appendix A
Appendix B	Endnotes
Abbreviations	Glossary
Bibliography	Acknow-ledgements
Illustration credits	Index
Blank or Imprint page	

13.1.1 *Type style and size in endmatter*

The same typefaces and styles as the main text are used.

As most of the endmatter material is for reference only it is usually set in a smaller size and with less leading than the main text.

The need to set an index within a fixed extent may require the index type size to be further reduced.

13.2 Appendices

13.2.1 *Numbering of appendices*

Style 1   Appendices are numbered: Appendix 1; Appendix 2; Appendix 3; etc.

Style 2   Appendices are numbered: Appendix I; Appendix II; Appendix III; etc.

Style 3   Appendices are numbered: Appendix A; Appendix B; Appendix C; etc.

In all cases, each appendix starts on a new page.

13.2.2 *Setting of appendices*

Style 1   Appendices are set in the same style and size as the main text.

Style 2   Appendices are set smaller than the main text.

Style 3   Appendices are set smaller than the main text and in two columns.

13.2.3 *Position of appendices*

Style 1   The appendices start on the first recto following the main text.

Style 2   The appendices follow a part-title at the end of the main text. The part-title carries the titles of the appendices: e.g. Appendices I–IV.

13.2.4 *Titles of appendices*

Style 1   The headings of the appendices are set in the same style as the chapter titles (see 7.3 *Chapter headings*).

Style 2   The headings of the appendices are set smaller than the chapter titles.

See also 12.3.15 *Preliminary pages.*

13.3 Bibliographical lists

13.3.1 *Bibliography, further reading and references*

Bibliographical lists may be presented in various forms:

bibliography – a bibliography is a list of material consulted by the author in the course of researching and writing a book or article. This list is usually placed in the endmatter at the end of the book. A bibliography may be divided up into chapters or subjects if this is helpful to the reader.

If the book consists of a collection of essays or articles, a bibliography for each may be placed at the end of the relevant piece.

select bibliography and **further reading** – in general non-fiction works, a bibliography may be edited down to a Select Bibliography, or the author may choose to produce a list of Further Reading.

references – in academic or scholarly works, a bibliography may be used in conjunction with footnotes or endnotes to give accurate references to works cited by the author. See 14.2–6 *Notes, Sources and References*.

The following is a guide to setting bibliographical lists for the general reader. For further information on creating complex bibliographies, see *New Hart's Rules* (OUP) and Judith Butcher, *Copy-editing* (CUP). For academic works, use the appropriate style guide (see 14.8).

13.3.2 *Styles of general bibliography*

Style 1   A bibliography, in alphabetical order, is placed in the endmatter.

Style 2   A bibliography, divided into chapters or subjects, is placed in the endmatter.

Style 3   A bibliography, divided into chapters, is placed at the end of each chapter.

Style 4   A Select Bibliography is placed in the endmatter.

Style 5   Further Reading is placed in the endmatter.

13.3.3 *Order of entries*

Style 1   Entries are listed in alphabetical order using author, or editor, surnames. Where multiple publications by one author are listed, they appear in alphabetical order of titles, excluding definite and indefinite articles.

Style 2   Entries are listed in alphabetical order using author, or editor, surnames. Where multiple publications by one author are listed, they appear in chronological order.

13.3.4 *Order of entries by multiple authors*

Where a publication is by multiple authors, follow the order given on the title page of the publication. The first author's name is used to place the entry alphabetically.

If the principal author also has solo publications listed, the solo works are listed before those written with other authors, regardless of alphabetical or chronological order.

13.3.5 *Order of elements within entries*

Style 1   For publications: author, *title*, [edition,] city, [publisher,] date
For articles: author, 'article title', *journal*, volume, city, [publisher,] date

Style 2   For publications: author, date, *title*, [edition,] city, [publisher]
For articles: author, date, 'article title', *journal*, volume, city, [publisher]

Elements in square brackets are not always listed.

NOTES TO 13.3.5

The above lists contain only the basic elements found in bibliographical lists of printed works. Other information may include: editor, translator, translated title, number of volumes, series title, etc. See *Hart's Rules* and Butcher's *Copy-editing* for further details on compiling entries.

Style 1 is usually preferred in general publishing and the humanities.
Style 2 is preferred in scientific publishing.

13.3.6 *Titles within entries*

Rule **Titles and sub-titles of publications are in italics. Article titles are in roman.**

Style 1 **Article titles take single quotation marks:**

Spender, S., 'Upward at Ninety', *Times Literary Supplement* (10 September 1993).

Style 2 **Article titles take double quotation marks:**

Spender, S., "Upward at Ninety", *Times Literary Supplement* (10 September 1993).

13.3.7 *Punctuation within entries*

Style 1 **Elements are separated by commas:**

Humfrey, P., *Glasgow Museums: The Italian Paintings*, London, 2012.

Style 2 **Elements are separated by commas, except for the place of publication and date, which are placed in round brackets:**

Humfrey, P., *Glasgow Museums: The Italian Paintings* (London, 2012).

13.3.8 *Full points ending entries*

Style 1 **Each entry ends with a full point:**

Humfrey, P., *Glasgow Museums: The Italian Paintings*, London, 2012.
Northcote, J., *The Life of Sir Joshua Reynolds*, 2nd edn, London, 1818.

Style 2 **Each entry does not end with a full point:**

Humfrey, P., *Glasgow Museums: The Italian Paintings* (London, 2012)
Northcote, J., *The Life of Sir Joshua Reynolds*, 2nd edn, London, 1818

NOTE TO 13.8.6
Titles of publications and articles should be treated as quotations and should not be altered in any way to match the editorial style of the main text.

13.3.9 Punctuation of names

The author's surname is given first, followed by the initials.

Style 1   Initials take a full point:

Crowe, J. A. and Cavalcaselle, G. B., *Titian: His Life and Times*, London, 1877.

Style 2   Initials do not take a full point:

Crowe, J A and Cavalcaselle, G B, *Titian: His Life and Times*, London, 1877.

13.3.10 References to multiple-volume publications and later editions

The number of volumes of a multi-volume work is given in Arabic numerals. The edition number is listed only if it is not the first.

Style 1   The elements are separated by commas:

Northcote, J., *The Life of Sir Joshua Reynolds*, 2nd edn, 5 vols, London, 1818.

Style 2   The elements are separated by commas; the edition number is in parentheses:

Northcote, J., *The Life of Sir Joshua Reynolds*, 5 vols, London, 1818 (2nd edn).

Style 3   Edition number, volumes, city and date are in parentheses:

Northcote, J., *The Life of Sir Joshua Reynolds* (2nd edn, 5 vols, London, 1818).

If citing a particular volume, this is given in roman numerals, followed by the volume title:

Penny, N., *The Sixteenth Century Italian Paintings*, vol. II, *Venice 1540–1600*, London, 2008

13.3.11 Series titles

The name of the series is given in roman upper- and lower-case:

Penny, N., *The Sixteenth Century Italian Paintings*, vol. I, *Paintings from Bergamo, Brescia and Cremona*, National Gallery Catalogues, London, 2008.

13.3.12 *Publisher and place of publication*

Style 1 **Just the place of publication is listed:**
Humfrey, P., *Glasgow Museums: The Italian Paintings* (London, 2012).

or:

Humfrey, P., *Glasgow Museums: The Italian Paintings*, London, 2012.

Style 2 **The place of publication and publisher are listed, separated by a colon:**
Humfrey, P., *Glasgow Museums: The Italian Paintings* (London: Unicorn Press, 2012).

or:

Humfrey, P., *Glasgow Museums: The Italian Paintings*, London: Unicorn Press, 2012.

13.3.13 *Editors and translators*

Style 1 **The name of the editor or translator is preceded by 'ed. 'or 'trans.':**
Haydon, B. R., *The Diary of Benjamin Robert Haydon*, ed. W. B. Pope, 5 vols, Cambridge MA, 1960–63.

Chion, M., *Jacques Tati*, Paris, 1987, English translation: *The Films of Jacques Tati*, trans. Viñas, M., Toronto, 1997.

Style 2 **The name of the editor or translator is followed by '(ed.)' or '(trans.)':**
Haydon, B. R., *The Diary of Benjamin Robert Haydon*, W. B. Pope (ed.), 5 vols, Cambridge MA, 1960–63.

Chion, M., *Jacques Tati*, Paris, 1987, English translation: *The Films of Jacques Tati*, Viñas, M. (trans.) Toronto, 1997.

13.3.14 *Listing online sources*

Style 1 **URL addresses are indicated by angled brackets. The date on which the author accessed the site is also given:**
'Guidelines on the Organizational Structure of Communist Parties', adopted at the Twenty-fourth Session of the Third Congress of the Communist International, 12 July 1921 <http://www.marxists.org/history/international/comintern/3rd-congress/organisation/guidelines.htm> (accessed 21 October 2013).

Style 2   URL addresses are set without brackets. The date on which the author accessed the site is also given:

'Guidelines on the Organizational Structure of Communist Parties', adopted at the Twenty-fourth Session of the Third Congress of the Communist International, 12 July 1921, http://www.marxists.org/history/international/comintern/3rd-congress/organisation/guidelines.htm (accessed 21 October 2013).

Care should be taken with long URL addresses that need to be divided between lines. The division should be placed after a slash with no extra hyphens added:

www.kcl.ac.uk/artshums/depts/history/study/handbook/assessment/taught/HistoryStyle Guide2.pdf

References to online material may be placed in a separate section to printed matter, if appropriate.

13.3.15 *Listing manuscripts*

The name of the manuscript collection is in roman.

The title of the individual manuscript is in roman, in quotation marks. If the manuscript has no title, just a description – such as diary – this does not take quotation marks.

The order of elements is:
author, title or description, date, location, collection, identification number

Letter from Giovanni Ambrogio Mazenta to Cassiano dal Pozzo, 12 May 1630, Rome, Biblioteca dell'Accademia Nazionale dei Lincei e Corsiniana, dal Pozzo MS VI (4) fol. 258r–v.

Description of the Doccia di S. Filippo (Shower of St Philip) sent to Cassiano by Bernardino Capitelli, 1634, Montpellier, Bibliothèque de l'École de Médecine, MS H.170, fol. 57r–v.

13.4   Glossaries

13.4.1   *Type styles in glossaries*

Style 1   Headwords are set in semi-bold or bold with definitions in regular:

Medium a fluid binder in which coloured pigments are suspended to make paint.

Macro and micro photographs magnified and highly magnified details of a painting or paint sample.

Style 2   Headwords are set in small caps with definitions in regular:

MEDIUM a fluid binder in which coloured pigments are suspended to make paint.

MACRO AND MICRO PHOTOGRAPHS magnified and highly magnified details of a painting or paint sample.

Style 3   Headwords are set in italic with definitions in regular:

Medium a fluid binder in which coloured pigments are suspended to make paint.

Macro and micro photographs magnified and highly magnified details of a painting or paint sample.

13.4.2   *Layout styles in glossaries*

Style 1   Entries are set with space between (usually about 2 mm):

Medium a fluid binder in which coloured pigments are suspended to make paint.

Macro and micro photographs magnified and highly magnified details of a painting or paint sample.

Millboard manufactured painting support made of compressed fibres bound with glue or oil and sometimes faced with paper.

Style 2   Entries are set with space between – this can be smaller than Style 1 – and the first line hung out to the left:

Medium a fluid binder in which coloured pigments are suspended to make paint.

Macro and micro photographs magnified and highly magnified details of a painting or paint sample.

Millboard manufactured painting support made of compressed fibres bound with glue or oil and sometimes faced with paper.

Style 3   Entries are set as a table, with the headwords in a column and the definitions in a column. There is space between entries:

Medium	a fluid binder in which coloured pigments are suspended to make paint.
Macro and micro photographs	magnified and highly magnified details of a painting or paint sample.
Millboard	manufactured painting support made of compressed fibres bound with glue or oil and sometimes faced with paper.

Style 4   Entries are set with the headword on a line by itself and the definition on the line below. There is space between entries:

Medium
a fluid binder in which coloured pigments are suspended to make paint.

Macro and micro photographs
magnified and highly magnified details of a painting or paint sample.

Millboard
manufactured painting support made of compressed fibres bound with glue or oil and sometimes faced with paper.

13.5 Indexes

Indexes are set in columns – usually two, three or four on a page – within the text panel. The text is set ranged left and may be smaller than other parts of the endmatter.

Style 1   Leave one line space between each letter of the alphabet:

Russia 205–6, 208, 211, 275, 357
Rydell, Dan 68–70, 80
Rylance, John 327, 336, 539

Sackville, Peter 370
St Malo 390–91
St Moritz 207

Style 2   Use an intitial between each letter of the alphabet:

Russia 205–6, 208, 211, 275, 357
Rydell, Dan 68–70, 80
Rylance, John 327, 336, 539

S

Sackville, Peter 370
St Malo 390–91
St Moritz 207

13.5.1 *References to illustrations in indexes*

Style 1   Indicate illustrations with italic page numbers:

Russia 205–6, 208–10, *211*, 275, 357
Rylance, John 327, *328*, 539

Style 2   Indicate illustrations with bold page numbers:

Russia 205–6, 208–10, **211**, 275, 357
Rylance, John 327, **328**, 539

13.5.2 Sub-entries and turned over lines

Style 1 Turned over lines indented 1 em; sub-entries indented 2 ems; turned over sub-entries indented 3 ems:

Lime Street 432, 491

London 39, 82–4, 86, 102, 109, 137–8,
 140, 195, 236, 260, 355, 369, 397, 407,
 439, 515
  British Museum 92, 213
  Broadcasting House 119
  Grosvenor Square 221, 225–7
   244, 251, 442, 514
  Museum Street 220
  Victoria Station 214
London Review of Books 120, 167, 282,
 420, 466

Style 2 Turned over lines from main entries and sub-entries indented 2 ems; sub-entries indented 1 ems:

Lime Street 432, 491

London 39, 82–4, 86, 102, 109, 137–8,
 140, 195, 236, 260, 355, 369, 397,
 407, 439, 515
 Broadcasting House 92, 213
 Dorchester Hotel 119
 Grosvenor Square 221, 225–7
  244, 251, 442, 514
 Museum Street 220
 Victoria Station 214
London Review of Books 120, 167, 282,
 420, 466

NOTE TO 13.5.2
The advantages of Style 2 are that it reduces the number of indents, and that the sub-entries hang out to the left of the turned over lines, making them easier to see.

13.6 Picture credits/sources

13.6.1 *Organisation of picture credits*

Style 1 Each illustration is listed in order of appearance, with copyright owner and/or photographer:

Fig. 5. © Devonshire Collection, Chatsworth / Reproduced by permission of Chatsworth Settlement Trustees / Bridgeman Images

Fig. 6. Wadsworth Atheneum Museum of Art, Hartford, CT

Fig. 7. © The Trustees of the British Museum. All rights reserved

Fig. 8. Vatican Museums and Galleries, Vatican City / Bridgeman Images

Fig. 9 © Mark Smith

Style 2 Each copyright-owning institution is listed, grouped geographically. Page numbers (or fig. numbers) are given for the illustrations:

HOUSTON
© The Menil Collection, Houston, photo Hickey-Robertson, Houston: p. 22

INDIANAPOLIS
© Indianapolis Museum of Art, Indiana: p. 143

LONDON
© The British Museum: pp. 90, 138

© The National Gallery, London: pp. 2, 13, 14, 20, 23, 27–9, 31, 33–41, 45, 46, 48–54, 57–66, 69–72, 75, 76, 79, 81, 85–8, 92, 93, 96–112, 116, 118–25, 129, 131–4, 137, 139, 140, 142, 143

© Royal Academy of Arts, London: pp. 25, 26

13.6.2 *Credits in multiple columns*

Style 1 Picture credits are set in two columns.

Style 2 Picture credits are set in three columns.

NOTE TO 13.6
Copyright-owning institutions may request particular wording in photographic credits. This should be agreed when images are licensed for use.

13.6.3 *Type style of picture credits*

Style 1   Picture credits are set in the same font as the main text, in a smaller size:

Fig. 6. Wadsworth Atheneum Museum of Art, Hartford, CT
Fig. 7. © The Trustees of the British Museum. All rights reserved
Fig. 8. Vatican Museums and Galleries, Vatican City / Bridgeman Images

Style 2   Picture credits are set smaller than the main text, and in a different font (e.g. the same font as the captions):

Fig. 6. Wadsworth Atheneum Museum of Art, Hartford, CT
Fig. 7. © The Trustees of the British Museum. All rights reserved
Fig. 8. Vatican Museums and Galleries, Vatican City / Bridgeman Images

13.6.4 *Layout of picture credits*

Style 1   Picture credits are set ranged left with space between them:

Fig. 7. © The Trustees of the British Museum.
All rights reserved

Fig. 8. Vatican Museums and Galleries, Vatican
City / Bridgeman Images

Fig. 9 © Mark Smith

Style 2   Picture credits are set ranged left with the figure number hung out to the left:

7   © The Trustees of the British Museum.
All rights reserved

8   Vatican Museums and Galleries, Vatican
City / Bridgeman Images

9   © Mark Smith

13.7 Endmatter in multi-volume works

Endmatter, such as appendices and the index, is placed at the end of the final volume. Using footnotes or chapter endnotes – rather than endnotes in the final volume – will allow the reader to check the references without having to consult a different volume.

NOTES, SOURCES AND CROSS-REFERENCES

References in general publishing

The subject of this chapter is the typographic treatment of notes, sources and references within a non-fiction text. The styles listed are those most often used in books aimed at a general readership. For academic publishing see 14.8 *References in academic publishing*.

14.1 Notes in general non-fiction

Notes are used to convey information that may be useful to the reader but would be distracting placed in the main text, such as:

sources of quotations   **biographical details**

historical background   **translations of foreign words or phrases**

In fictional works they may be added by an editor or translator to explain the context of older or translated texts. In general non-fiction, three forms of notes are commonly used:

footnotes – placed at the bottom of the relevant page

chapter endnotes – placed at the end of the relevant chapter

endnotes – placed in the endmatter

14.1.1 *Footnotes and endnotes*

Style 1   Footnotes, set at at the bottom of the page, are used

Style 2   Endnotes, set at the end of the chapter, are used

Style 3   Endnotes, set in the endmatter, are used

14.1.2 *Combining footnotes and endnotes*

It is possible to use both footnotes and endnotes together in the same publication. Endnotes are used for sources, etc.; footnotes to give information that the reader may need as they are reading, e.g. translations of foreign words. See 14.2.1 *Numbering footnotes*.

NOTE TO 14.1
Sidenotes, set in the fore-edge margins, require large margins and a great deal of attention from editor and designer. They are not often used in general non-fiction.

14.2 Footnotes

Footnotes are indicated by a superior number or symbol placed in the text. The numbered note is placed at the foot of the page:

1608–1679) made efforts to apply Galileo's laws of dynamics to the movements of the stars.[14] The pioneering work of Galileo came to flower and to fruit in the hands of Isaac Newton (1642–1727), whose *Principia Mathematica*

---

14. He also, impressed by the new successes of mathematics applied to the mechanics of moving inanimate objects, attempted to apply mathematics to the processes of living organisms. At any rate in the domain of movement and muscular forces, he succeeded in discovering some new principles in this field.

For setting superior figures, see 14.4 *Note indicators*.

14.2.1 Numbering footnotes

Style 1 Footnotes are numbered consecutively throughout the whole publication.

Style 2 Footnotes are numbered starting from 1 in each chapter or section.

Style 3 Footnotes are numbered starting from 1 on each page.

Style 4 Footnotes are indicated with footnote symbols in the following order:

* † ‡ § ¶ ‖ ** †† ‡‡ §§ ¶¶ ‖‖

starting from * on each page:

* The footnotes of history.
† Fonds Jourquin.
‡ General Bonaparte was often called 'Le Petit Tondu', the little man with the close-cropped hair.
§ Louis Madelin, *Vers l'Empire d'Occident*.

If combining footnotes and endnotes (see 14.1.2) use Style 4 for footnotes and superior numbers to indicate the endnotes.

14.3   Endnotes

The styles below may be applied to chapter endnotes or to endnotes. Chapter endnotes are placed at the end of the chapter, under the main text with the heading Notes. Endnotes are placed in the endmatter (see 13.1 *Order of endmatter*).

14.3.1   *Numbering endnotes*

Endnotes are indicated by a superior figure placed in the text.

Style 1   Endnotes are numbered consecutively throughout the whole publication.

Style 2   Endnotes are numbered starting from 1 in each chapter or section. The Notes section is divided into sub-sections with headings.

14.3.2   *Layout of endnotes*

Endnotes are set smaller than the main text.

All three Styles below may be set with the text justified or ranged left, depending on how the main text is set. If using narrow columns it is acceptable to set the endnotes ranged left to avoid uneven word-spacing. See examples opposite.

Style 1   The numbers are hung out to the left and ranged left.

Style 2   The numbers are hung out to the left and ranged right.

Style 3   The notes are ranged left with vertical space between them. There is a full point between the number and the note.

14.3.3   *Notes in a double-column layout*

In large-format publications, endnotes may be set in two columns to save space and to avoid having too many characters per line.

Style 1   Endnotes are set in a single column.

Style 2   Endnotes are set in a double column.

Styles for 14.3.2

Style 1

96   Bignami Odier 1981, p. 101.

97   Bignami Odier 1973, p. 197.

98   Ubrizsy Savoia 1980, p. 132, stated that 'he was originally from L'Hérault'.

99   Fully transcribed in B.II, p. 62.

100 Paris, IF, *Catalogue de la bibliothèque botanique de Mr. Benj. Delessert*, MS 7136, fol. 27.

101 For Delessert's life, see De Coninck 2000.

102 Candolle 1799–1803.

103 In 1799, for example, Delessert purchased the large herbal of Jean and Nicolas Laurent Burmann, though it was only shipped to Paris in 1810: Lasègue 1845, pp. 65–7; Hoquet 2002, p. 105.

104 Hoquet 2002, p. 101.

105 Ibid., pp. 102ff.

106 Lasègue 1845, p. 46.

107 Guillemin 1825.

Style 2

96   Bignami Odier 1981, p. 101.

97   Bignami Odier 1973, p. 197.

98   Ubrizsy Savoia 1980, p. 132, stated that 'he was originally from L'Hérault'.

99   Fully transcribed in B.II, p. 62.

100 Paris, IF, *Catalogue de la bibliothèque botanique de Mr. Benj. Delessert*, MS 7136, fol. 27.

101 For Delessert's life, see De Coninck 2000.

102 Candolle 1799–1803.

103 In 1799, for example, Delessert purchased the large herbal of Jean and Nicolas Laurent Burmann, though it was only shipped to Paris in 1810: Lasègue 1845, pp. 65–7; Hoquet 2002, p. 105.

104 Hoquet 2002, p. 101.

105 Ibid., pp. 102ff.

106 Lasègue 1845, p. 46.

107 Guillemin 1825.

Style 3

96. Bignami Odier 1981, p. 101.

97. Bignami Odier 1973, p. 197.

98. Ubrizsy Savoia 1980, p. 132, stated that 'he was originally from L'Hérault'.

99. Fully transcribed in B.II, p. 62.

100. Paris, IF, *Catalogue de la bibliothèque botanique de Mr. Benj. Delessert*, MS 7136, fol. 27.

101. For Delessert's life, see De Coninck 2000.

102. Candolle 1799–1803.

103. In 1799, for example, Delessert purchased the large herbal of Jean and Nicolas Laurent Burmann, though it was only shipped to Paris in 1810: Lasègue 1845, pp. 65–7; Hoquet 2002, p. 105.

104. Hoquet 2002, p. 101.

105. Ibid., pp. 102ff.

106. Lasègue 1845, p. 46.

107. Guillemin 1825.

14.4 Note indicators

14.4.1 *Setting numbers as indicators*

Footnotes and endnotes are usually indicated by superior figures placed in the text. It is possible to change the font of superior figures, giving the typesetter the choice between using lining or non-lining figures (if both are available in the chosen typeface). Non-lining figures may give the appearance of bobbing up and down:

$$\text{wax}^1 \quad \text{wax}^3 \quad \text{wax}^6 \quad \text{wax}^7 \quad \text{wax}^8 \quad \text{wax}^9$$

Style 1 Note indicators are set in the same font as the text using non-lining figures:

were the Quakers[16] and Unitarians[17] who had helped make Birmingham 'the City of a Thousand Trades'.[18] He was a

Style 2 Note indicators are set in the same font as the text using lining figures:

were the Quakers[16] and Unitarians[17] who had helped make Birmingham 'the City of a Thousand Trades'.[18] He was a

Style 3 Note indicators are set in a different font:

were the Quakers[16] and Unitarians[17] who had helped make Birmingham 'the City of a Thousand Trades'.[18] He was a

14.4.2 *Multiple note indicators*

If two notes apply to the same text, they are separated by commas:

from the English when the *Bellerophon* was searched.[26, 27]

If three or more sequential notes apply to the same text, the indicators are set as follows:

from the English when the *Bellerophon* was searched.[26–9]

14.4.3 *Placement of indicators*

Rule   The indicator is placed at the end of the sentence, unless referring to specific words within the sentence. The indicator is set outside punctuation (except dashes) unless the note refers to the final word of a sentence or a phrase inside parentheses.

Rule   If possible, avoid placing indicators next to numbers where they may cause confusion.

14.4.4 *Notes without indicators*

If the notes give details of references to sources, etc., but do not contain information that is essential to the reader, they may be set as endnotes without indicators within the text. This simplifies the look of the page of text.

The notes are set with a page number and the relevant quotation from the text.

Style 1   The quotation is set within quote marks:

p.360   'No man can . . .' Suzanne Hayes, Adelaide March 1984
p.362   'a penny a pound too much . . .' *Paths of Progress: A History of Marlborough College*, Thomas Hinde (James & James, 1992), 189
p.363   'We set off . . .' 25.7.55, Marlborough College archive
p.364   'She was a . . .' *On the Black Hill*, 219

Style 2   The quotation is set in a heavier font, bold or semi-bold:

p.360   **No man can . . .** Suzanne Hayes, Adelaide March 1984
p.362   **a penny a pound too much . . .** *Paths of Progress: A History of Marlborough College*, Thomas Hinde (James & James, 1992), 189
p.363   **We set off . . .** 25.7.55, Marlborough College archive
p.364   **She was a . . .** *On the Black Hill*, 219

These notes can only have the page numbers inserted after the main text has been set and the pagination fixed; time for this process should be built into the schedule.

14.5 Sources

The following section gives some of the methods for citing sources within a general non-fiction text. Other methods may be used in academic publications and by certain specialisms (see 14.8.1 *Academic style guides*).

14.5.1 *Citing sources in full*

If sources are given in full, the elements are placed in the same order as in a bibliography (see 13.3 *Bibliographical lists*) with the relevant page numbers at the end. The one difference is that the author's initials are set before the surname:

C. Walker, 'Learning to Draw in Rome: the Role of Art Schools', in *Renaissance Drawings*, New York, 2015, p. 31

Style 1   The full source is placed in parentheses in the main text:

inspire similar books printed in Italy (C. Walker, 'Learning to Draw in Rome: the Role of Art Schools', in *Renaissance Drawings*, New York, 2015, p. 31). With the growing interest in Roman art

Style 2   The full source is placed in a footnote or endnote.

14.5.2 *Short-form citations*

When a text contains extensive references, a short-form system such as the *author–date* system may be used. A shortened form of the source – surname of author, date of publication, page numbers – is used in the text:

Walker 2015, p. 31

At the end of the text, a list of references gives the short and full sources in an alphabetical list (see 14.6.4 *List of references*):

Walker 2015
C. Walker, 'Learning to Draw in Rome: the Role of Art Schools', in *Renaissance Drawings*, New York, 2015, p. 31

Style 1	The short-form source is placed in parentheses in the main text:

inspire similar books printed in Italy (Walker 2015, p. 31). With the growing interest in Roman art in England during the first half of the seventeenth century and an increased

Style 2	The short-form source is placed in a footnote or endnote.

14.5.3 *Author–date system*

In the author–date system, the reference to a published source is abbreviated to the author, date and page number:

Walker 2015, p. 31

If the author has published two or more articles or books in a year, lower-case letters are used to distinguish them:

Walker 2015a, p. 31
Walker 2015b, p. 56

If the publication has two authors, both are named:

Style 1	Walker & Yeats 2015, p. 31

Style 2	Walker/Yeats 2015, p. 31

If the publication has three or more authors, *et al.* is used after the first author:

Walker *et al.* 2015, p. 56

The page number(s) may be indicated with a 'p.' or 'pp.'

Style 3	Walker 2015, p. 31

or separated from the year by a colon:

Style 4	Walker 2015: 31

14.5.4 *List of references*

If using one of the short form systems, place a list of references in the endmatter, or at the end of the relevant article. The styles in this section show ways of treating these entries, using the author–date system as an example.

A designer may adapt these depending on the design of the publication and the space available. It is important that the reader can locate entries easily, so the short forms should be clear.

In the first three styles, the short form is set on a line above the entry. There is space between entries. The type styles used are:

regular:

Style 1   Coulter 1996
J. Coulter, 'The Notorious Polly Davis', *Norwood Past*, London 1996.

David 2011
J. David, 'Zoffany's Painting Technique: *The Drummond Family* in focus' in *Johan Zoffany RA*, ed. M. Postle, New Haven 2011.

semi-bold:

Style 2   **Coulter 1996**
J. Coulter, 'The Notorious Polly Davis', *Norwood Past*, London 1996.

David 2011
J. David, 'Zoffany's Painting Technique: *The Drummond Family* in focus' in *Johan Zoffany RA*, ed. M. Postle, New Haven 2011.

small caps:

Style 3   COULTER 1996
J. Coulter, 'The Notorious Polly Davis', *Norwood Past*, London 1996.

DAVID 2011
J. David, 'Zoffany's Painting Technique: *The Drummond Family* in focus' in *Johan Zoffany RA*, ed. M. Postle, New Haven 2011.

In the next three Styles, the short form is set, followed by a colon, then the entry. The second and third lines are indented:

Style 4 Coulter 1996: J. Coulter, 'The Notorious Polly Davis', *Norwood Past*, London 1996.
David 2011: J. David, 'Zoffany's Painting Technique: *The Drummond Family* in focus' in *Johan Zoffany RA*, ed. M. Postle, New Haven 2011.

Style 5 **Coulter 1996**: J. Coulter, 'The Notorious Polly Davis', *Norwood Past*, London 1996.
David 2011: J. David, 'Zoffany's Painting Technique: *The Drummond Family* in focus' in *Johan Zoffany RA*, ed. M. Postle, New Haven 2011.

Style 6 COULTER 1996: J. Coulter, 'The Notorious Polly Davis', *Norwood Past*, London 1996.
DAVID 2011: J. David, 'Zoffany's Painting Technique: *The Drummond Family* in focus' in *Johan Zoffany RA*, ed. M. Postle, New Haven 2011.

In the final three Styles, the short form is set in a colum on the left with the entries in a wide column on the right:

Style 7 Coulter 1996   J. Coulter, 'The Notorious Polly Davis', *Norwood Past*, London 1996.
David 2011   J. David, 'Zoffany's Painting Technique: *The Drummond Family* in focus' in *Johan Zoffany RA*, ed. M. Postle, New Haven 2011.

Style 8 **Coulter 1996**   J. Coulter, 'The Notorious Polly Davis', *Norwood Past*, London 1996.
David 2011   J. David, 'Zoffany's Painting Technique: *The Drummond Family* in focus' in *Johan Zoffany RA*, ed. M. Postle, New Haven 2011.

Style 9 COULTER 1996   J. Coulter, 'The Notorious Polly Davis', *Norwood Past*, London 1996.
DAVID 2011   J. David, 'Zoffany's Painting Technique: *The Drummond Family* in focus' in *Johan Zoffany RA*, ed. M. Postle, New Haven 2011.

14.6 Abbreviations in notes

14.6.1 *Frequently cited people and institutions*

If the name of a person or institution is repeated many times in the notes, it may be shown in an abbreviated form. A list of abbreviations is given in the endmatter before the references or bibliography:

BAV	Vatican, Biblioteca Apostolica Vaticana
Florence, BNC	Florence, Biblioteca Nazionale Centrale
Montpellier, BEM	Montpellier, Bibliothèque de l'École de Médecine

14.6.2 *Repeated references*

Ibid. (short for *ibidem*) means 'in the same place' and may be used if a note contains a reference to the same work as the previous note.

12. Whistler 2015, p. 31
13. Ibid., p. 35
14. Ibid., p. 38

14.7 Cross-references within a text

14.7.1 *Page references*

Style 1   The abbreviated 'p' or 'pp' is set with a full point, followed by a space, then the number:

p. 45   pp. 78–9   p. 119   pp. 421–30

Style 2   The abbreviated 'p' or 'pp' is set with a full point, closed up to the number:

p.45   pp.78–9   p.119   pp.421–30

Style 3   The abbreviated 'p' or 'pp' is set without a full point, followed by a space, then the number:

p 45   pp 78–9   p 119   pp 421–30

Rule   Page references in the main text are set within parentheses:

(see pp. 64–6)   (see pp.64–6)   (see pp 64–6)

14.7.2 *References to illustrations*

References in the text to illustrations can take the forms:

Fig. 35 (short for figure)
Pl. 35 (short for plate)
Cat. 35 (short for catalogue number)

The plurals of these – Figs, Pls, Cats – do not take full points.

The reference is placed in parentheses in the main text.

Style 1   'Fig.' and the number are set with a word-space:

(Fig. 19)   (Pl. 19)   (Cat. 19)

Style 2   'Fig.' and the number are set closed up:

(Fig.19)   (Pl.19)   (Cat.19)

Rule   The plural forms are set with a word-space:

(Figs 19 and 20)   (Pls 19–21)   (Cats 19, 20 and 22)

Rule   The illustration is placed close to, but after its reference in the text.
Any further references to the illustration, later in the text, use 'see':

(see Fig. 19)   (see Pl. 19)   (see Cat. 19)

14.7.3 *Chapter/article references*

References to other chapters or articles within a publication will
depend on the form of headings being used.

Style 1   In a book divided into chapters:
(see Chapter 3)

Style 2   In a book with multiple authors:
(see Whistler & Yeats)

Style 3   In a book divided into numbered subsections:
(see 12.6.2)

14.8 References in academic publishing

Academic publishing is a highly specialised field, with each subject area having its own set of conventions concerning the display of material and, in particular, the correct method for referring to sources. It would be impossible in a book this size to describe all of these in detail – the list of titles opposite provides a starting point for those working with academic texts.

14.8.1 *Academic style guides*

Many academic journals publish their own style guides. While these are primarily written for the journals' contributors, they provide a good reference for authors and editors working within the same subject matter.

Style guides can cover a wide range of concerns that are relevant to the creation of scholarly and scientific texts, such as:

preparation of the manuscript – including the treatment for headings, bylines, citations/references, figures and tables

use of language – including spelling, grammar, punctuation, capitalisation

legal and ethical issues – including the responsibility of the authors, intellectual property, conflict of interest and libel

technical terminology – including nomenclature, abbreviations, units of measurement, statistics

work processing – including submission procedure, marking up of proofs

Universities and other educational institutions often produce a style guide document for students writing theses or dissertations. These are usually provided online for free.

A selection of academic style guides and manuals:

general
New Hart's Rules: The Oxford Style Guide (Oxford University Press, 2nd edition, 2014)

Butcher's Copy-editing: The Cambridge Handbook for Editors, Copy-editors and Proofreaders (Cambridge University Press, 4th edition, 2006)

The Chicago Manual of Style: The Essential Guide for Writers, Editors and Publishers (University of Chicago Press, 16th edition, 2010)

medical
AMA Manual of Style: A Guide for Authors and Editors (OUP USA, 10th edition, 2009) – from the American Medical Association

social sciences
Publication Manual of the APA (American Psychological Association, 6th edition, 2009)

science
Scientific Style and Format: The CSE Manual for Authors, Editors, and Publishers (University of Chicago Press, 8th edition, 2014) – from the Council of Science Editors

The ACS Style Guide: Effective Communication of Scientific Information (OUP USA, 3rd edition, 2006) – from the American Chemical Society

humanities
MLA Style Manual and Guide to Scholarly Publishing (Modern Language Association, 3rd edition, 2008)

MHRA Style Guide: A Handbook for Authors and Editors (Modern Humanities Research Association, 3rd edition, 2013)

law
Oscola: The Oxford University Standard for the Citation of Legal Authorities (Hart Publishing, 4th edition, 2012)

The Bluebook: A Uniform System of Citation (Harvard Law Review Association, 20th edition, 2015) – compiled by Harvard Law Review Association, the Columbia Law Review, the University of Pennsylvania Law Review, and the Yale Law Journal.

For more reference books see the *Bibliography*, p. 268

Corporate style

CORPORATE STYLE

15.2 Office branding

15.2.1 *Stationery – correspondence and memos*

The standard format for a letterhead for use with office printers is A4. The following information may be included:

company name/logo
company address
company phone number (direct line and/or general)
e-mail address (direct or general)
company website address
directors' names
registered company/charity number

Letterheads can be pre-printed with the above information. The office can also purchase unprinted A4 sheets of the same paper. These are called 'continuation sheets' and may be used for pages 2, 3, etc.

If letterheads are created as digital templates, the above information is printed out on the office printer as the letter is printed. This allows for individual telephone numbers and e-mail addresses to be added at negligible additional cost. They can also be easily amended.

15.2.2 *Stationery – invoices*

Invoices can also be pre-printed or digital templates. They may carry these additional elements, or space for them:

invoice date	payment/account details
invoice number	terms of payment
customer reference number	VAT number
purchase order number	

Invoices can be set up within an accounting or spreadsheet program that will add the items and calculate VAT automatically. Larger companies may have systems set up for printing invoices that protect against fraud.

The majority of invoices are now produced digitally and e-mailed.

Whether letterheads are pre-printed or digital templates, the style of text used for letters should be consistent throughout the organisation.

Word-processing programs allow less tweaking than design programs, which creates a challenge when trying to design an attractive and legible page of text. The main factors to consider are:

choice of font – choose a font that has been designed for setting body text and is available on all computers in the organisation.

type size – the size of type should be chosen visually, not according to a formula.

leading – if you are using a word-processing program which does not allow small adjustments to leading, the choice is likely to be between single-line spacing, one-and-a-half-line spacing and two-line spacing. Which one you choose will depend on the chosen text font.

margins – to be adjusted according to type size and length of line. The print area of the office printer will have a bearing on this.

alignment – the text can be set either justified or ranged left.

paragraph breaks/indents – new paragraphs are indicated either by an indent, or by a line space, but not both.

A detailed discussion of these points can be found in the introduction to body text (see p. 29).

Samples of the template in use should be provided by the designer as a visual guide.

Ideally the design of the text to be used in letters should be determined in conjunction with the design of the stationery. Style sheets can be set up within the word-processing program to speed up the formatting of the text.

NOTE TO 15.2
A template contains a page grid for the layout of text and images and style sheets for the formatting of text.

15.4 Sales and marketing

15.4.1 *Supplying advertisements to other publications*

Printed publications that include advertising will supply specifications for companies wishing to buy space:

size – dimensions are given for available spaces: e.g. full-page, vertical half-page, horizontal half-page, quarter-page. If bled-out full pages are available, the spec should include the trimmed page size and the bleed.

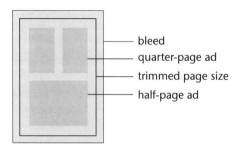

bleed
quarter-page ad
trimmed page size
half-page ad

type area – for bled-out ads, the publication may suggest a limit on how close to the edge of the page text may be placed.

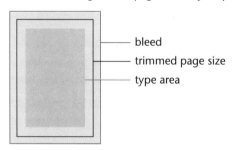

bleed
trimmed page size
type area

colour or black and white – colour ads must be supplied with colours created in CMYK for print.

output – the standard resolution for printed material is 300 DPI. High-res PDF is the most common type of output, but others may be acceptable. Formats are usually specified by the publication.

Advertising space comes in a wide range of shapes and sizes and this should be considered with care during the design process to ensure that all advertising is visually consistent.

Decide what information is necessary in all ads, and which can be left out of the smaller sizes.

The size of online ads is usually given in pixels rather than millimetres and DPI.

15.4.2 *Sales brochures and catalogues*

Sales material, such as brochures and catalogues, may include the following:

company information	price list
contact details	terms and conditions
product information	order form and/or sales contact

A brochure can be expensive to produce. A larger print-run is more economical. Consider how long the brochure will be used for and whether some information could be published separately. For example, if the product line is updated annually, but the price list is updated quarterly, it would make sense to print the price list as a separate sheet, thus prolonging the life of the brochure.

See *Appendix C* for guidance on production.

15.4.3 *Order forms*

Order forms can be complex documents and should be laid out as simply and as clearly as possible, using a legible font.

Ensure that there is adequate space for customers to write their own details and that the form is printed on paper which can absorb ink without smudging. Coated papers do not provide a good surface for ink pens.

15.6.5 *Running feet in magazines*

The running foot should contain the folio, the title of the magazine, the issue number (if applicable) and/or the publication date:

48 | LONDON CITY GARDENS | ISSUE 27

15.6.6 *Regular items in magazines*

Items which appear in every issue of a magazine, such as the Editor's Introduction and Letters to the Editor, should be placed in the same position and styled in the same way in each issue.

15.6.7 *The mast-head*

The *mast-head* of a magazine, made up of its title in a decorative typeface sometimes with a drawn element, should be treated consistently in each issue. The colours of the mast-head may be changed to match the image on the front cover or to mark successive issues.

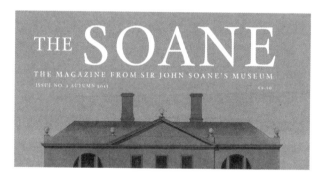

15.6.8 *Newsletters*

A newsletter, be it of a national corporation or a local group, should have a distinctive typeface for its mast-head. Repeat issues using the same style of layout reinforce the standing and authority of an organisation:

15.6.9 *Advertising space for sale*

The size of advertising spaces will depend on the grid used throughout the magazine. Advertisements may be grouped together in a section or, more usually, distributed throughout the publication. A specification sheet should be created for advertisers supplying artwork and sent at the earliest opportunity. This should include:

dimensions of ads – making clear which is the height and which is the width. If full-page bled-out ads are available, the trimmed page size and the bleed should be given.

printing – colour (CMYK) or black and white, required resolution of images and type

acceptable file types – for example, PDF, high res TIF

deadline for artwork – and details of how and where to send files

proofing details – will the advertiser receive a proof of their ad before printing?

Appendices

APPENDICES

APPENDIX B

Printing and finishing

Printing methods

An understanding of the basic processes and terms used in printing will be necessary when work is being specified for a printer.

There are two methods of printing used for publications: offset lithography, referred to as *litho* printing, and digital printing.

litho – offset litho printing gives a better quality result and is more economical for medium and long runs. A wider range of papers and formats may be used. Litho printing offers a full range of printing in colour, black only or black with a *spot colour*.

digital – digital printing is more economical for short runs between 10 to 200 copies. Digital printers will usually carry a smaller choice of papers and may have a limited number of finished paper sizes. Four-colour and single-colour jobs can be printed. Digital printing is improving both in quality and its capacity to use a wider range of paper sizes and weights. The future may see it compete comprehensively with litho printing.

Printing colours

colour printing – colour is produced by the process of using four inks – cyan (blue), magenta (red), yellow and black; the combination is referred to as 'CMYK'. In litho printing this is achieved by using four separate printing plates, one for each of the four ink colours. The digital system does not use separate plates but uses the the simultaneous deposition of four coloured pigments.

special or spot colours – these are made by mixing inks to produce a colour which can be replicated accurately. The industry standard is achieved by mixing the inks using the Pantone® colour system. This ability to repeatedly produce a specific colour is important in the commercial branding of products, brochures, leaflets and packaging.

greyscale – black and grey images are produced by dots of black ink. Such images are referred to as *greyscales* or *half-tones*.

Sending document output to printers

Once the design, text and layout is approved – signed off – by the publisher, it is output. There are two mechanisms of ouput. In one the work is sent to the printer in the the file created by the layout program, such as Adobe InDesign®, along with any images. The other process is to make a high res **print-quality PDF** to the printer's specification. This is now the standard form of output.

Proofing

There are four types of proofs:

high resolution proofs – for checking colour, text and image quality. The proof paper is either coated or matt to match the paper that will be used. These proofs are an accurate representation of the final print quality and are used to match the colours on press.

scatter proofs – these are high res proofs containing the images only on a large sheet. These can be done before the layout is completed so the process of correcting the colours can start.

PDF proofs – for checking content and layout on screen. The final print quality of coloured images cannot be judged solely on their appearance on screen.

inkjet or laser proofs – the quality is not of a high resolution and they are only used for checking content and the sequence of the pages. These are produced imposed, folded and collated. They are referred to as *plotters*.

wet proofs – in this process printing plates of selected pages are made and printed on press using the chosen paper. This is the absolute test of colour and print quality. Wet proofs add significantly to cost so are rarely used.

Which sort of proofs are chosen depends on the needs of the project and the available budget. If in doubt, ask the printer for advice. Be aware that colours will appear differently on a screen, which is RGB and fluorescent, and on the page printed CMYK. Different papers will also create variations in colour.

Adjusting the colour values

Unless you have experience in making adjustments to colour values of CMYK and greyscale images, this is best left to the photographer, or to the printer's repro department.

Corrections and revisions

If textual errors are spotted after the printer's proofs are reviewed, corrections can be made. If output has been by application file, the printer can be asked to carry out minor text corrections. If a PDF output has been used, a PDF of any revised pages is supplied and the printer replaces those pages. In both these cases PDFs of the corrected pages must be seen to confirm the correction.

If the reproduction of coloured images is not satisfactory, adjustments to colour values can be made. This is a specialist area for the printer's repro department to undertake. Further high-resolution proofs are produced to confirm the changes. Once that is done, the work is ready for the press.

Paper choices

When choosing paper for printing books and periodicals the factors are:

paper surface – papers and cards are either *coated*, having a smooth shiny surface formed by a mineral film or *uncoated*, with no additional material on the paper fibres. A coated paper will give a truer representation of colour images. Coated papers can be matt, silk or gloss. Matt papers produce less glare and are less tiring when reading long texts.

colour – a bright white page allows for the best colour reproduction yet may produce visual dazzle with black text. Off-white or cream paper makes for a more comfortable background for long black-only texts as in novels.

weight – heavier papers will create a thicker and heavier book and have less *show-through*, that is, when the text printed on the other side of the page can be seen. A larger page will require a heavier paper.

textures – some card covers and papers are produced with a textured surface. These can be used to add interest to printed objects.

Print finishes

There is a wide range of finishes that may be applied to printed sheets, covers and book jackets during or after the printing process:

sealer – a clear coating that is applied as part of the print run to give the printed sheet a smooth finish. It also reduces ink drying times.

varnishes – are used to apply a gloss or matt finish to card or paper.

laminates – these are clear coatings applied to card covers. They give matt, satin, gloss or 'soft-touch' finishes.

spot varnishes – varnish applied to a selected area of the page, such as an illustration or to specific lettering on a cover to make it stand out.

foil – the application of coloured or metallic film to selected areas or text on paper, card or cloth covers.

Additional processes can be applied to printed card or paper:

embossing/debossing – a shape or lettering impressed into card.

die-cutting – shapes cut out of card or paper using a cutting form.

Binding methods

Books, booklets, brochures and periodicals are printed on large sheets of paper, usually containing 16 pages (8 per side). Folded into sections called *signatures* they are then collated into the finished sequence.

The following methods are used for binding:

saddle-stitched – binding using metal wire staples. The most commonly used method for short publications. The number of pages and the paper weight may limit this process to no more than 64 pages.

perfect binding – binding in which the pages are glued along the spine, and the whole is then glued into card covers.

thread-sewn – binding in which the pages are sewn in signatures, glued along the spine, then glued into card covers or hard boards.

case bound – binding in which the pages are either perfect bound or thread-sewn in sections to create a *book-block*. The *case* is made up of a front and back board joined by a flexible cloth or cloth-substitute spine. The case is covered by paper, cloth or leather. The book-block is attached to the boards by a paper sheet, the *endpaper*, glued front and back. The spine of the book may have a square back or a rounded back.

self cover – the front and back cover are printed on the same paper as the inner pages, folded and saddle-stitched. No card is needed for the cover which reduces costs. It is commonly used for newsletters, short brochures and local magazines.

APPENDIX C

Marking up proofs

Use a mark at the point of the correction and a combination of symbols and words in the margin to explain the change. To avoid any possible confusion it is always better to write out the instruction in full.

A fine red pen is best for marking up; light grey pencil will not show up clearly on a photocopy or when scanned for digital transmission.

Below are the commonly used marks to texts:

Mark	Marked text	Corrected text	Instruction
#	The harvest every year	The harvest every year	insert space
⌐⌐⌐	my aunt was fond of glass	my aunt *was* fond of glass	to italics
⌐⌐	I am *keeping* the clocks	I am keeping the clocks	to roman
⋀ i	certan times of the day	certain times of the day	insert character
trs	She came to twice us	She came to us twice	transpose words
≡	And, unlike you, jim does	And, unlike you, Jim does	to a capital
⌡	care abоut persistence	care about persistence	close up
stet	I washed my few dishes	I washed my few dishes	ignore correction
⊙	of water The stone walls	of water. The stone walls	insert full point
ᛌ	the great lake therefore	the great lake, therefore	insert comma
fit	I suppose, to me it	I suppose, to fit me it	insert word
✑	my uncle could the find it	my uncle could find it	delete word
⌡	spoiled girl from the city	spoiled girl from the city	extra space
;	late April a great event	late April; a great event	insert semi-colon
⊙	views mirrors refract light	views: mirrors refract light	insert colon
⊙	It is true of the past	It is true of the past?	insert question mark

NOTE

The British Standards Institute publishes a comprehensive list of copy marks: *Guide to Copy Preparation.*

①	Except I am alive│	Except I am alive!	exclamation mark
⸜ ⸝	│I'll do it⸝ James said	'I'll do it', James said	insert single quotes
⸜ ⸝	│I'll do it⸝ James said	"I'll do it", James said	insert double quotes
⊢⊣	north/facing windows	north-facing windows	insert hyphen
N̲	touched them ┤ made me	touched them – made me	use en dash
⊙	forward...then back	forward . . . then back	use spaced ellipsis
⸘	and forty years old.2̲	and forty years old.²	use superior figure
	and forty years old.2̸	and forty years old.²	use superior figure
?	Uncle Sideny sat down	on-going query – resolve with the editor

Changes to capitalisation and font styles are also marked up:

s/c	My uncle could find	MY UNCLE could find	change to small caps
U/l	IN AUGUST the men	In August the men	to upper and lower case
c/s	You are keeping one	YOU ARE KEEPING one	to caps/small caps
≢	in the Seventh Century	in the seventh century	to lower case
	in whose house did it	in **whose** house did it	change to bold
wf	who stood at his side	who stood at his side	wrong font, change
lig	at what inefficiency	at what inefficiency	use ligature

If the correction is complex or cannot be easily explained using a symbol, spell it out and circle it:

(Would it be better in bold ?)

Where a particular word or phrase occurs many times in a text, it may be speedier to use the global **find and change** process by which the change is done throughout the entire document. Care has to be taken if the replacing word is longer or shorter and might disrupt lines of the existing typesetting.

Changes to spacing, leading, indentation and typesetting are shown overleaf.

Defining typeface sizes

Type sizes are measured in points – approximately 72 points to an inch.

The visual size of a printed character is dependent on two values: the point size and the x-height. The point size is measured from the top of the ascender to the bottom of the descender. The x-height is the height of the lower-case letter 'x':

Stone sans   Trinité   Bodoni   Bembo   Minion   Gill sans   Rialto

The x's from the above example, all in 18 pt: X X X X X X x

Thus the instruction to 'use 12 point type' will not necessarily produce text that looks the same size as a previous setting in 12 pt if the typeface is different.

The relationship between the x-height and leading

Variable x-heights have an effect on the spacing of the lines, the 'leading' required to produce readable lines of text (see p. 29). Both the samples below are in 10 point and 'set solid', that is 10 point type with 10 point leading:

Rialto
> He had dreamt once of writing novels, but had not achieved so much as a novella, in spite of all the unfinished manuscripts lying around in folders. But unfinished they were fated to remain, he having been unlucky with his muses, they, for some reason, having never tarried long enough in his

Minion
> He had dreamt once of writing novels, but had not achieved so much as a novella, in spite of all the unfinished manuscripts lying around in folders. But unfinished they were fated to remain, he having been unlucky with his muses, they, for some

The Rialto example requires no extra leading, but the Minion needs extra leading of at least 3 pts to make the text easily readable:

> He had dreamt once of writing novels, but had not achieved so much as a novella, in spite of all the unfinished manuscripts lying around in folders. But unfinished they were fated to remain, he having been unlucky with his muses, they, for some

The set and fit of typefaces

The width of characters in a typeface and the way they are designed to fit together affects the overall printed appearance. Both the visual size and the space occupied on a line may vary as these examples show:

Rialto 12 pt	quaint wooden latticework
Garamond 12 pt	quaint wooden latticework
Times NR 12 pt	quaint wooden latticework
Cycles 12 pt	quaint wooden latticework
Sabon 12 pt	quaint wooden latticework

Sabon 9.5 pt	He had dreamt once of writing novels, but had not achieved so
Scala 9.5 pt	He had dreamt once of writing novels, but had not achieved so
Rialto 9.5 pt	He had dreamt once of writing novels, but had not achieved so

If the extent of a publication is fixed, the choice of typeface may be limited to those that allow a large number of words per page while still maintaining readabilty. An experienced designer can advise on this.

Roman and italic typefaces

A roman serif typeface is the conventional face for continuous text. The horizontal strokes of the base serifs are thought to help the eye along the line.

Italics are used for emphasis, quotations, book titles, foreign words and sometimes internal dialogue.

Their behaviour here is making life *intolerable*.

The Times noted that the absence of *The Adoration of the Magi* lessened the impact.

was an *imaret* (soup-kitchen for the poor) or a *hamam* (public bath)

For ten years now people have been asking me, *Are those your teeth?* Each time, before they ask *Are those your teeth?* they say *Excuse me.* They don't like the fact that they're my teeth.

If the text is set in italic, that which would have appeared in italic is set in roman, the *opposite font*:

> *The scene opposite shows the visitors looking at Watteau's* Les Noces *or* L'accordée du Village *through the gallery's doors.*

Small capitals

These are capitals in a reduced size, drawn to have the same weight as capital letters. They have many uses – in subheadings, capitalised words in continuous text, running heads or feet (as at the bottom of this page) or chapter openings:

MAIN HEADING

SUB-HEADING

THAT SEPTEMBER, IN PARIS, I STARTED AT THE LYCÉE Henri-IV, in the preparatory *classe de philosophie*, as a full-time

For capitalised words in continuous text:

> from Tangier was also mistakenly delivered to me instead of to my father: URGENT SETTLE FLAT RENT AT ONCE STOP it read

They are used in abbreviations in continuous text:

> in the first century BC the people

Small caps benefit from letterspacing: SEPTEMBER   SEPTEMBER

Semi-bold and bold typefaces

These are heavier versions of a typeface:

semi-bold   *semi-bold italic*   **bold**   ***bold italic***

They are used in lists, indexes, tables and commercial reports as highlights:

Metro, Moscow **55–6**, 245–6   here to indicate pages with illustrations
Mikoyan, Anastas **206**, 284
Mikoyan, Stepan 20, 176, **177**, 178–9, **180**

Resources expended	**2013/4**	here to indicate dates
Buildings	369,420	
Visitor Services	814,674	
	1,184,094	here to indicate totals

Superscript and subscript figures

Superscript (or superior) figures are commonly used as indicators to footnotes or endnotes:

> Ensconced with his relic far from prying eyes in a mansion guarded by the militia and N.K.V.D.,[28] Zbarsky reported to the Government that his 'project' was 'in a very good state'.[29]

It is possible to increase or decrease the size of the superscript figure in typesetting programs. They are important in academic texts and the size should be increased; more informal works benefit from a smaller, less intrusive size:

> Only 3 per cent of men born in 1923 made it beyond 1945.[62] increased

> 'With Raskova, of course!' Irina's mother retorted.[62] reduced

The superscript figure should be placed after any punctuation. Superscript numerals are more easily read if set in lining figures.

For texts with only occasional footnotes, an asterisk is sufficient. If there are more on a single page, a sequence of other symbols is used:

> from a single * to † ‡ § ¶ **

Subscript figures are used in chemical formulae and mathematical works:

$$H_2O \quad C_2N_5OH \quad H_2SO_4$$

Ligatures

The fit of one character to another is fixed in the type design process. With some combinations, notably with the letter **f** this may cause an ugly clash and special combinations called ligatures are devised to overcome this:

> fi ff fl ffl ffi in ligature form: fi ff fl ffl ffi

Some languages have other ligature combinations: fj ss to fj ß

Some ligatures can be found in the glyph table (see 10.2.2). Not all fonts have a complete set of ligatures.

Sans-serif typefaces

If using a sans-serif font for text setting, choose one that has a good range of fonts. This example is Stone Sans:

roman lower-case	abcdefghijklmnopqrstuvwxyz
roman capitals	ABCDEFGHIJKLMNOPQRSTUVWXYZ
roman non-lining and lining figures	1234567890 1234567890
roman small caps	ABCDEFGHIJKLMNOPQRSTUVWXYZ
italic lower-case	abcdefghijklmnopqrstuvwxyz
italic capitals	ABCDEFGHIJKLMNOPQRSTUVWXYZ
italic non-lining and lining figures	1234567890 1234567890
semi-bold lower case	abcdefghijklmnopqrstuvwxyz
semi-bold capitals	ABCDEFGHIJKLMNOPQRSTUVWXYZ
semi-bold non-lining and lining figures	1234567890 1234567890
semi-bold small caps	ABCDEFGHIJKLMNOPQRSTUVWXYZ
semi-bold italic lower case	abcdefghijklmnopqrstuvwxyz
semi-bold italic capitals	ABCDEFGHIJKLMNOPQRSTUVWXYZ
semi-bold italic non-lining and lining figures	1234567890 1234567890
bold lower-case	abcdefghijklmnopqrstuvwxyz
bold capitals	ABCDEFGHIJKLMNOPQRSTUVWXYZ
bold non-lining and lining figures	1234567890 1234567890
bold italic lower-case	abcdefghijklmnopqrstuvwxyz
bold italic capitals	ABCDEFGHIJKLMNOPQRSTUVWXYZ
bold italic non-lining and lining figures	1234567890 1234567890

If you are using a serif typeface and a sans-serif in the same publication, choose faces that are similar in their proportions. Some fonts are designed to be used together in this way, for example, Scala and Scala Sans:

abcdefghijklmn   abcdefghijklmn

Using sans-serif typefaces

A sans-serif typeface may be unsuitable for book-length texts, but can be used for shorter texts in advertisements, company reports and displayed headings. In this book, where the text is divided into short statements, a sans-serif was chosen to distinguish the text from the examples.

When a sans-serif is used, increasing the leading will aid readability:

RESOURCES

The Archive collections comprise around 8 million items relating to the historic environment, 60% of which are photographs dating from the 1850s to the present day.

. 7 on 8.5 pt

RESOURCES

The Archive collections comprise around 8 million items relating to the historic environment, 60% of which are photographs dating from the 1850s to the present day.

7 on 10.5 pt

Reversing out type

Reversing out type refers to the use of white lettering aganst a darker background.

White on black background
Text set in small type sizes are difficult to read.
Using a bolder typeface makes for easier reading.

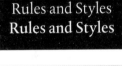

White type on coloured backgrounds
White texts set over a lightly coloured background may become illegible.

Coloured type on illustrations
This may result in portions of the lettering becoming barely discernable.

Type choices
Avoid using typefaces with very fine lines.
This is especially important with lettering printed over a four-colour image. The finer elements may become blurred to the point of disappearing.

APPENDIX F

Abbreviations, contractions and acronyms

Abbreviations

Strictly these are words created by omitting the last part of a word and placing a full point afterwards:

> century to cent.   association to assoc.   lieutenant to lieut.
> General to Gen.   Admiral to Adm.   Captain to Capt.
> dots per inch to d.p.i.   post meridian to p.m.

Contractions

These are formed by removing the letters in the middle of the word:

> Doctor to Dr   Saint to St   Mister to Mr   Reverend to Revd

Acronyms

These are formed by using the initial letters of a group of words, usually of organisations:

> British Broadcasting Corporation to BBC
> North Atlantic Treaty Organisation to NATO

Honours and titles are also formed as acronyms:

> OBE   CBE   MBE   MVO   DBE   OM   CH

The use of full points between letters is dealt with in section 3 *Punctuation*.

Avoid Latin abbreviations, unless they are common in the field in which you work:

> *vide infra* to see below   *viz* to namely   *inter alia* to among others

The contraction of 'and' to the ampersand '&' should be avoided unless it is part of the proper name of a company.

No apostrophe is needed for the plural of acronym. The possesive apostrophe is used in the normal way:

> OBEs   DBEs   an MP's function   NATO's forces

Unfamiliar acronyms should be preceded by the names spelled out at the first mention. Thereafter the acronym alone is used:

> A report from the National Institue for Health and Care Exellence (NICE) has been submitted. Responses to NICE's comments were

Commonly used abbreviations

a.m. ante meridian
b. born
ca. c. about
cf. compare to/with
d. died
e.g. for example
et al. and others (of persons)
etc. and so on
fig., figs figure, figures
fl. flourished
i.e. that is
no., nos number(s) note that 'nos' has no full point
p., pp. page(s)
pl. plural
p.m. post meridian
pt., pts part(s)
trans. translator, translated by
% always use 'per cent' except in financial reporting

for weights and measures:
£ pound
lb pound
oz ounces
mm millimetre
cm centimetre

kg kilogram
l. litre
p.p.m. parts per million
d.p.i. dots per inch
mph miles per hour

for bibliographical use:
abr. abridged
app. appendix
art. article
bull. bulletin
chap., chaps chapter(s)
col., cols column(s)
ed., eds edited by, editor(s)
fasc. facsimile
fol. folio
n., nn. note(s)
n.d. no date
n.p. no price, no publisher
par., pars paragraph(s)
repr. reprint
sec., secs section(s)
ser. series
supp. supplement
v., vv. verse(s)
vol., vols volume(s)

NOTE
The New Oxford Dictionary for Writers and Editors gives the meanings for lesser-known abbreviations

Preparing word-processing documents for typesetting

Preparing text files in a word-processing program

It is standard practice in the publishing industry for text files to be written and edited in a word-processing program, such as Microsoft Word, and then converted into a layout program, such as InDesign for typesetting. A consistent text file can make this process quicker and reduce the number of errors that may be introduced.

Paragraph indents and line breaks
Use consistent indent spacing throughout the text to indicate new paragraphs: a tab *or* a first-line indent *or* a line space. Whatever indent spacing is used, it should be consistent throughout the text.

Using a mixture of indent spacing will create more work for the typesetter as they will have to be searched for line by line.

If a text file has been created with line spaces for paragraphs, and these are to be removed and replaced with indents, note this when supplying the text.

Where line spaces are to be retained as section breaks, make it clear by using an instruction like this – [[line #]] – in the text file.

New pages
Page breaks should be put into the text file only where a new page is required in the final setting. Page breaks should be put in using the appropriate page break command. Do not create a new page with a large number of line returns. A keyed-in instruction [[new page]] can also be used to make this completely clear.

Headings and sub-headings
Standardising the style for each level of heading in the text file will make it easier for the designer to apply their chosen styles. Instructions may be placed in the text file to indicate A-level headings and B-level headings, etc., if requested by the typesetter:

> Saxon Houses [A]
> Saxon house construction [B]

Footnotes and endnotes

Word-processing programs set and number footnotes automatically. Instructions should be given for how they are to be set and numbered in the final document (see 14.3 *Footnotes*).

Where possible, avoid late changes to note sequences as they may not always be automatically renumbered in the typesetting program. If a chapter's endnotes are cut and pasted into a combined endnote section, the links to the chapter are disconnected and any changes to numbering will have to be made manually.

Illustration placement

If figure references appear in the text, e.g. (Fig. 4), highlighting them in the file like this **(Fig. 4)** will help the designer place the images. If there are to be no figure references in the text, an instruction [[Fig. 4]] tells the designer where an image should be placed. The instruction is then deleted from the text. If image instructions in the text are long [[put Fig. 4 here at a quarter page, don't crop the top]], removing them will cause re-flow of the text, which may affect the layout. It is better to supply a separate list of image treatments.

Cross-references

References to pages elsewhere in the publication are numbered after the text is set. A placeholder like this (see p.ooo) is used temporarily. If coloured it it easier to spot and less likely to be missed in the later stages of proofreading.

Italics and small caps

Ensure that styles such as italics and small caps are applied only to the chosen words and not to the adjacent punctuation.

Accents and special sorts

Not all fonts have a complete range of accented characters. Warn the designer if a text contains any unusual accents or special sorts.

Tracked changes

If tracked changes have been used in the editorial process, accept the changes before sending the final text to the designer or typesetter. If the text is sent without the tracking changes accepted and transferred into a typesetting program the result is unreliable and therefore unusable.

Further reading and reference books

Reference books are updated regularly, so the following list does not include dates or edition numbers. Get the latest edition you can afford.

Book Typography: A Designer's Manual, Michael Mitchell and Susan Wightman, Libanus Press

Cassell's Dictionary of English Grammar, James Aitchison, Cassell & Co

The Chicago Manual of Style, University of Chicago Press

Copy-editing, Judith Butcher, Cambridge University Press

The Economist Style Guide, ed. John Grimond, Profile Books Ltd

The Effective Editor's Handbook, Barbara Horn, Pira International

The Elements of Style, W Shrunk Jnr and E B White, Longman

The Elements of Typographic Style, Robert Bringhurst, Hartley & Marks Publishers

Fowler's Dictionary of Modern English Usage, Jeremy Butterfield, Oxford University Press

Guardian Style, David Marsh and Amelia Hodson, Guardian Books

Guide to English Style and Usage, compl. by Tim Austin, Times Books

New Hart's Rules, Oxford University Press

New Oxford Dictionary for Writers and Editors, Oxford Universtity Press

New Oxford Spelling Dictionary, ed. Maurice Waite, Oxford Universtity Press

The Penguin Guide to Punctuation, R L Trask, Penguin Reference Books

The Picture Researcher's Handbook, Hilary and Mary Evans, Routledge

Style Manual for Authors, Editors, and Printers, AGPS Press

Usage and Abusage: A Guide to Good English, Eric Partridge, Penguin Books

Online reference

Some house style guides are available online as downloadable PDFs or Word documents:

University of Oxford style guide:

www.ox.ac.uk/sites/files/oxford/media_wysiwyg/University%20of%20
Oxford%20Style%20Guide.pdf

Cambridge University general style guidelines:

https://authornet.cambridge.org/information/academic/downloads/
General%20style%20guidelines.pdf

House styles for American publications may be useful:
CUP has such a Style Sheet:

www.cambridge.org/us/.../Cambridge_style.doc

Some style guides are for specific texts such as dissertations:
www.kcl.ac.uk/artshums/depts/history/study/handbook/assessment/taught/
HistoryStyle Guide2.pdf

line-spacing
see 'leading'

lining figures (modern) 21, 72
set of figures which are all the same
height and set 1234567890
   note indicators 210
   in tables 91
see also 'non-lining figures'

list of illustrations 176

lists
   numbered lists 83–4
   punctuation of 82

litho (offset lithography) 240
printing from metal plates using oil-based
inks and water

liturgies 138–9
   instructions to the public 138–9
   setting of hymns 139

logotype 155, 157, 165, 223
   sponsor's logo 173

loose 33, 41
setting with wide spaces between the words,
or with large spaces between the lines

lower-case 19
the standard non-capitalised alphabet
   roman numerals 78–9
   with non-lining figures 72

magazines 232–4
   articles 232
   mast-head 234
   pull quotes 232–3
   running feet 234
   templates 232
   type styles 232

main text 150
the main portion of the book without
prelims or endmatter
   pagination 94
   size 40

manual adjustments to text
the manipulation of a text setting, line by line,
to improve word-spacing and appearance
   repeated hyphens 43
   repeated words 43

manuscripts
   listing in bibliography 193

maps 120, 178–9

margins 18, 151
unprinted areas around the text panel
   accessibility 262
   captions in 127
   magazines 232
   marking up proofs 244
   office stationery 225
   poetry 132

marketing
see 'sales and marketing'

mast-head 234
displayed title of magazine

matt paper 242
paper with a non-reflective surface finish

measure 23
width of a text panel
   character width 32, 38
   justified text 32, 43
   narrow measure 38
   type size 40

measurement, units of 75

medium 37
weight of font, sometimes equivalent to
'regular', sometimes equivalent to
'semi-bold', depending on the typeface

modern figures
see 'lining figures'

moiré effect 121
unwanted visual effect that can occur
when images made of fine dots or lines
are printed

money 73

multi-column layouts
see 'columns'

multiplication sign 75

repro (reproduction) 121, 241–2
the process by which the final layout and
artwork is converted into printing plates

reproduction rights 116–17
the legal right to reproduce a text or image

resolution 117, 121, 228, 235, 239, 242, 247
number of pixels in a given area of a digital
file. High resolution files are suitable for
printing

reversed out 147, 257, 262–3
white type (unprinted paper) on a black or
coloured background

RGB (red, green, blue) 223, 248
colours out of which digital images are
produced on a computer screen

roman 20, 50, 253
upright form of a typeface
    opposite font 51

roman numerals 21, 78–9
set of numerals devised by the
Romans I II III IV V VI VII VIII IX X

rotation of pages 84, 179

royal 150
a standard book format,
approx. 234 x 153 mm

rules
printed straight lines
    with running heads 112
    in tables 88–9

running feet 112
book or chapter title repeated at the
bottom of every page
    in magazines 234
    when to delete 110

running heads 110–12
book or chapter title repeated at the
top of every page
    content of 111
    placement 110
    reference works 112
    rules used with 112
    type style 110
    when to delete 110

run-on
following directly on from previous text
    poems 135

run-on chapters 94–5
chapters that do not start a new page but
follow on below the previous chapter

saddle-stitch 243
binding method using metal staples to
secure pages and cover together

sales and marketing 228–9
    brochures 229
    order forms 229
    supplying advertising 228

sans-serif 19, 256–7, 263
letterforms with no serifs
    body text 29, 36
    captions 122, 126

scanning 116, 247
process of rendering artwork into a
digital image

scatter proofs 241
proofs of illustrations on a large sheet

screen 121
pattern of dots out of which four-colour
images and half-tones are printed.

script 19
typeface designed to resemble handwriting

section 45, 47
division of text when scene or subject
changes

section break (line break) 45
space of one or two lines in the text panel

section opening
see 'part-title'

select bibliography 188
a selection of publications used by an
author

self-cover 243
cover of publication printed on the same
sheet of paper as the text

semi-bold 20, 39, 51, 254
typeface with thicker strokes than a regular
face, though not as thick as a bold face

semi-colon
  punctuation of lists 57

sentence
  unfinished sentences 64

series 154
a range of books produced to the same format
and design

serif font 19
font with additional horizontal and oblique
strokes which terminate the main strokes of a
character
  body text 29

set 253
the width of characters in a font
  of lining and non-lining figures 91
  see 'character width'

set solid 22
text set with no leading

setting down 67
setting extracts at a smaller size than
the body text

short-form citation 212–13
a method of referring to sources, using a
shortened form of the information

show-through 242
printed text from one side of a page visible
on the reverse side

sidenotes 127, 204
notes set in a wider side-margin, usually
the fore-edge

signature 152
printed sheet, consisting of 8, 16 or 32 printed
pages, folded and trimmed to form a section
of the book

silk paper 242
coated paper with a slightly reflective
surface finish

small caps 20, 254
capitals reduced in size but with the same
weight as standard capitals
  in body text 52
  first line of chapter 108
  letterspacing 52
  with non-lining figures 72

sources 212–15
  author–date system 213
  citing in full 212
  list of references 214–15
  short-form citations 212–13

spacing *see* 'kerning', 'leading',
'letterspacing', 'tracking', 'word-spacing'

special sorts (special characters) 21, 38, 144
characters not commonly found in
Latin-alphabet fonts

specification
description of work to be carried out
  working to a fixed specification 153

speech
see 'dialogue'

speech attribution 64
phrase that tells the reader who is speaking

spelling out numbers 79
expressing numbers in words rather
than figures, e.g. 'five' rather than '5'

spine 156–7
the side of the book where the pages are
bound together

spot colour (special colour) 39, 223, 240
colour created by mixing inks, not produced
using four-colour process

spread 18, 132, 160
two pages opposite each other
  double-page spread 94, 117, 178–9

square brackets 50, 58, 68
brackets usually used to indicate an editorial
insertion [ ]
  in plays 130

typeface 19, 251–9
alphabet and related characters
drawn to one design
    set and fit 253
    sizes 252
    x-height 252
see also 'font'

typeface family 37, 251
group of faces based on one design,
but varying in weight and width

typescript (TS) 134, 136
printed-out copy of author's text file

type size 40
height measured in points from the top of
the ascender to the bottom of the descender
    body text 30, 40
    captions 122
    character width 30
    extent 40
    leading 31
    measure 40
    readability 40
    in tables 85
    weight 40
    words per page 40
    x-height 30

typographic style 10

uncoated paper 242
paper with no mineral coating

upper-case 19
capital letters
    in body text 52
    capitalising foreign words 145
    capitalising titles 166
    letterspacing 52, 259
    with lining figures 72
    roman numerals 78

verso 18, 94–5
left-hand page
    dual-language setting 146
    prelims 160
    running heads 111, 131

weight 20
thickness of strokes in the letterforms
    body text 39
    type size 40

weight of paper 240, 242–3
expressed in gsm (grams per square metre)

weights and measures 75

wet proofs 121, 241
proofs produced on press, on the
chosen paper

widow 47
the last line of a paragraph falling at
the top of a page

word division 44
splitting a word between the end of one line
and the start of the next, using a hyphen
    hyphenation settings 44
    methods of 44
    in ranged left setting 42

word processing documents
    preparing for typesetting 264–5

word-spacing 21
amount of space between the words
in a line of type
    in justified text 32–3, 43
    in poetry 136
    in ranged left text 33, 42

words per page 40

work progression 15, 238–9
procedure for completing a job

x-height 22, 252
height of the lower case x in a font, which
determines the visual size of a font
    character width 32
    leading 41
    type size 30, 40

MICHAEL MITCHELL is the founder of Libanus Press where he has been designing, publishing and occasionally writing books for forty years. He is a Fellow of the International Society of Typographic Designers and a former President of the Double Crown Club.

SUSAN WIGHTMAN studied at Ravensbourne College of Design and Communication and Exeter School of Art. She joined Libanus Press as a typographer in 1996.

They are co-authors of *Book Typography: A Designer's Manual* (2005).